"Always focus on doing what's right — for employees, for customers, and for society. If you do this, the results will come. Tom has written more than a book — he has condensed decades of leadership into a solid compendium for success in all aspects of life. Its lessons are timeless. I urge you to read and keep it at your deskside as a constant reminder of how life should be lived in all its aspects. It is Tom's best work, and following its wise counsel will change your life forever."

– Dr. Sylvio Dupuis
Former President of Notre Dame College and Catholic Medical Center
Former Mayor of Manchester, NH

"Is it possible for a book to be both powerful and practical? This book provides both while telling the story of how one organization not only survived, but thrived, during the COVID-19 pandemic. Your organization may still be struggling during these challenging times, but it isn't too late to learn how a leader and his team navigated unknown territory with agility and resilience to become an even better organization as judged by their customers, stakeholders, employees, and their community while improving bottom line performance and top line growth."

– Kay Kendall, CPHQ
CEO & Principal BaldrigeCoach
Former Judge for Baldrige Performance Excellence Program

"Twenty years ago, I first heard Tom Raffio say, 'If you take care of your customers and your people, the results will take care of themselves.' The solid, measurable success of Northeast Delta Dental, both before and during the COVID-19 pandemic, is a testament to the effectiveness of his leadership style and his uncompromising approach to Malcolm Baldrige principles of management. *Prepare for Crisis — Plan to Thrive* is a how-to guide for running a successful and sustainable organization."

– Richard Tango-Lowy
Master Chocolatier and Owner of Dancing Lion Chocolate

"This jewel of a book offers timeless lessons for any service organization on the true meaning and powerful impact of generosity. The lessons from Northeast Delta Dental before and during the pandemic capture the power of generosity in creating stakeholder trust, loyalty, and long-term success."

– Leonard Berry, Ph.D.
University Distinguished Professor of Marketing,
Mays Business School, Texas A&M University

"Tom's thoughtful book on leadership is important in all seasons and for all companies. Its insightful, yet practical, prescriptions have been road-tested by Tom with enormous success over twenty-five years at his company, including the pandemic. It is an important, engaging, and very timely read. He has earned deep and wide respect inside Northeast Delta Dental as well as in the broader community, where his positive impact is unceasing. At the end of the day, a successful leader's integrity, character, decency, and values do the most to inspire excellence in colleagues. By that measure, they just don't come any better than Tom Raffio. He personifies 'servant leadership', and his book demonstrates its success."

– John T. Broderick, Jr.
Former New Hampshire Supreme Court Chief Justice
Senior Director External Affairs for Dartmouth-Hitchcock and
advocate for its Mental Health Awareness Program

"This is an excellent, easy read, written by a caring leader who shows the pathway to success during a crisis. It demonstrates the importance of shared culture and values, teamwork, a detailed disaster recovery plan, and communication, communication, and more communication. My advice? Follow this template to adapt and thrive in hard times."

– Craig Goldsmith
DeltaVision Project/Product Manager

"This is a great book for young managers, future leaders, and anyone who wants to be successful in the service industry!"

– Dr. David Staples
Chair, Delta Dental Plan of New Hampshire

Prepare for Crisis — Plan to Thrive

The Inside Story of How One Company Did It Right

By failing to prepare,
You are preparing to fail.

- Benjamin Franklin

Prepare for Crisis — Plan to Thrive

The Inside Story of How One Company Did It Right

Tom Raffio
President & CEO of Northeast Delta Dental
with Diane Schmalensee
President of Schmalensee Partners

Dedications

This book was inspired by Daniel DeFoe's classic, *A Journal of the Plague Year*, and the unpublished COVID-19 emails from Dr. Joanne Conroy (CEO and President of Dartmouth-Hitchcock) to her employees and Board. It is dedicated to the amazing employees of Northeast Delta Dental, who strive every day to do their absolute best for their customers, dentists, and communities, and to our Board members, who give their enthusiastic, nimble, and unwavering support to their Northeast Delta Dental family.

This book is also dedicated to our biggest fans and spouses, Ellen and Richard, who were (mostly) understanding and supportive as we wrote and re-wrote this book at all hours, while promising that each version was the last. This really is the final version! Yes, really. We truly mean it this time!

Copyright Notice

This edition published 2021 by Tom Raffio and Diane Schmalensee

ISBN: 979-8-9852193-0-2 (paperback)
ISBN: 979-8-9852193-1-9 (e-book)

Contents

Introduction
This Book Is Written for Leaders Who Want to Be Prepared 9

Section 1
Before the Crisis: Build a Strong Foundation Based on the
Best Management Principles 13
    1. Have a Clear and Motivating Mission and Core Values 14
    2. Know Your Business 16
    3. Make Serving Your Customers a Top Priority 28
    4. Create a High-Functioning Board Using Best Governance Practices 30
    5. Establish Trusting Relationships with Legislators and Regulators 33
    6. Create a Robust Strategic Planning Process and Goals 34
    7. Plan Ahead for a Crisis — Build Resiliency 37
    8. Build a Strong Infrastructure 39
    9. Be a Servant Leader and Communicate, Communicate, Communicate ... 42
    10. Insist on Best Management Practices 45

Section 2
During the Crisis: Use the Foundation to Act Wisely 49
Realize There Is a Crisis 49
Prioritize Stakeholder Well-Being Over Profits 51
Get Board and Regulator Approval to Act 55
Communicate, Communicate, Communicate 57
Serve and Communicate with Employees 58
Communicate with the Board and Regulators 67
Serve and Communicate with Participating Dentists 68
Serve and Communicate with Customers 72
Serve and Communicate with Brokers and Benefit Consultants 74
Serve and Communicate with Communities 75

Section 3
**Emerging from the Crisis: Renew the Foundation
with Lessons Learned** 79
The Initial Recovery Process 80
Conclusions 86
    1. Base Crisis Response on Authentic Values 86
    2. Do Well by Doing What's Right 87
    3. Focus on the Long Term 89
    4. Adopt a "Level 5" Servant Leader Style 90
    5. Build Trust 92
    6. Embrace the Proven Baldrige Principles 94
    7. Be Ready for the Next Disaster 95
    8. Most Importantly, Strengthen the Foundation 97
What If It's Not Over? What If We Face Other Disasters? 98

Communications Appendix 103
    To Employees 103
    To Participating Dentists 117
    To Customers 122
    Public Blogs, Op-Eds, and Radio 127
    To Brokers and Benefit Consultants 131
    Message from the Black Heritage Trail of New Hampshire
    Executive Director 135

Acknowledgments 137
About the Authors 141
References Mentioned in This Book 145

Introduction

This Book Is Written for Leaders Who Want to Be Prepared

As I write this book, the COVID-19 crisis is well into its second year. Some organizations — especially those that require close human contact — have closed, some are cautiously emerging, and others are reopening to a changed world after adopting new and improved processes and technologies. And leaders everywhere are wondering how they can be better prepared to deal with the next inevitable crisis.

I'm writing this book for these current and future leaders. My goal is to share the story of how the organization I lead, Northeast Delta Dental, was challenged yet survived and even thrived in terms of our reputation, operational quality, and market position during the crisis. I hope this will offer hope and guidance so other organizations can do the same.

What do I mean by "crisis"? Of course, there are many dreaded possibilities in addition to the COVID pandemic. There are natural disasters such as floods, earthquakes, fires, or storms. There are nuclear, biological, and chemical attacks or accidents. There are people who commit crimes against our people or locations. There is the sudden, unexpected loss of a key person in the organization. My goal is to offer helpful insights that apply in all types of crises, drawing on my organization's experiences during the pandemic.

Saying that Northeast Delta Dental, a dental insurer serving Maine, New Hampshire, and Vermont, was challenged by the pandemic doesn't adequately express how hard it hit all the people we serve. That includes our employees, our participating dentists, our customers, our brokers, and our communities. Like many others, Northeast Delta Dental had to essentially close our physical offices and radically change in many ways. Even though we had already laid out a plan to address a pandemic, we didn't immediately recognize the seriousness of the crisis we faced and had to play catch up. Fortunately, because we had laid a strong foundation through good management and leadership practices, we were able to quickly get back on track and emerge strong.

Throughout the COVID crisis, our primary goal has not been revenues or financial gain. Instead, we have focused on relief for all our stakeholders and our communities that would be most beneficial to them, with their safety and health uppermost in our considerations. In 2020, we invested $27 million (about 8% of our annual revenue) in stakeholder relief, with none of the costs passed along to customers, and yet ended up financially strong. I firmly believe it's possible to perform well financially and operationally while doing good for others and that we become stronger when our stakeholders become stronger.

I learned a lot during this crisis and share this so you and other leaders will also be able to lead your organizations through crises and emerge stronger and more resilient than before.

I hope that, if you take away only one idea from this book, it is that a good foundation built on strong management and leadership principles is essential. Pandemics take a lot of energy and resources just to survive. Managing during a crisis is much easier if your organization has a foundation that supports, rather than diverts time and resources from, your response to the pandemic. Emerging successfully is much more likely if the foundation you have built speeds up your actions rather than slows them down. It all comes down to good common sense. If you go into a crisis in a strong position, you are much more likely to handle it well, be resilient, and emerge strong. If you go into a crisis weak or off balance, you will have a much bigger challenge and may be lucky to merely survive.

> *"If you go into a crisis in a strong position, you are much more likely to handle it well, be resilient, and emerge strong."*

This book is organized in three sections:

1. Before the Crisis: Build a Strong Foundation Based on the Best Management Principles
2. During the Crisis: Use the Foundation to Act Wisely
3. Emerging from the Crisis: Renew the Foundation with Lessons Learned

Section 1

Before the Crisis

Build a Strong Foundation Based on
the Best Management Principles

About This Section

This section describes in considerable detail how Northeast Delta Dental worked to build a strong foundation for our business. Everyone who knows me knows that I often say that success is the sum total of paying attention to the details. Details create the big picture for me and are essential to my systems thinking. I offer this detail so that those who want to undertake similar steps can understand what we did.

I know that not every reader will be interested in all this detail. If you are not, please pay careful attention to the main headings so you will be familiar with what I consider to be the essential elements of a strong business foundation. While the details are specific to Northeast Delta Dental, I've included them so readers can determine how they might apply — or apply with modifications — within their own organizations.

What are the elements of a strong business foundation? My list has developed over time through experience and study. I may have missed some important elements, but I believe that building these foundational elements helped Northeast Delta Dental come through the crisis in surprisingly good shape.

1. Have a Clear and Motivating Mission and Core Values
2. Know Your Business

3. Make Serving Your Customers a Top Priority
4. Create a High-Functioning Board Using Best Governance Practices
5. Establish Trusting Relationships with Legislators and Regulators
6. Create a Robust Strategic Planning Process and Goals
7. Plan Ahead for a Crisis — Build Resiliency
8. Build a Strong Infrastructure
9. Be a Servant Leader and Communicate, Communicate, Communicate
10. Insist on Best Management Practices

1. Have a Clear and Motivating Mission and Core Values

As the CEO of Northeast Delta Dental, I believe in the power of our mission and core values to guide our decisions and behaviors and to build strong relationships with everyone who contributes to our continued success — our customers, dentists, brokers, and ourselves. We developed our mission and values statements soon after I arrived in 1995. The Board, the management team, and our employees periodically review and update them as appropriate in Board and staff meetings and feedback sessions.

Once the statements are prepared and printed on posters, everyone physically signs them to affirm their commitment. These are more than the feel-good statements that many companies produce. They are our authentic values in our corporate DNA. One of the best compliments I've received came from a consultant who worked with us and met many employees. He said that walking into the Northeast Delta Dental offices felt like walking in a "fresh green forest" because he could feel the enthusiasm and positive tone everywhere—from the mail room to the board room.

Northeast Delta Dental's Informal Mission Statement

Everybody deserves a healthy smile.

Northeast Delta Dental's Formal Mission Statement

We advance the oral health and overall wellness of our customers and the general public by providing innovative benefits and professional partnerships through diversified strategic business and philanthropic initiatives.

Notice that our mission focuses on several things. First, it focuses on advancing the oral health of our customers and the general public (not only our customers). Second, it focuses on building professional partnerships with dental professionals, with brokers, and with other business organizations. Third, it focuses on diversifying our businesses, which we have done by adding new strategic businesses and products. Finally, a fourth focus is on being philanthropic.

Similarly, we defined our four core values with feedback from all our employees. Involving employees in the process helped them embrace, and be motivated by, the values.

Northeast Delta Dental's Four Core Values

1. We believe that effective **communication** is essential for our continued success as a great place to work and a stellar place to do business for all customers, service providers, and employees.
2. We believe that **teamwork** is key to working effectively toward our mission, being committed to giving 100%, and to working collaboratively with shared responsibility and accountability.
3. We believe that **quality** is a core value that enables us to strive continually toward reaching our mission and goals, and to achieving excellence in all that we do, resulting in our consistent feeling of pride in our work at Northeast Delta Dental.
4. We believe that **integrity** is a crucial value that enables us to be respectfully honest and responsive to internal and external customers.

We work within the pillars of our four core values, which help us balance profitability with social responsibility. By living the behaviors that support these shared values, I believe we can most effectively, consistently, and purposely achieve our corporate vision and strategic goals.

Time and time again, including during the COVID-19 pandemic, having clear values and goals has provided us with invaluable guidance on how to plan and act during a crisis.

2. Know Your Business

Northeast Delta Dental began in 1961 as New Hampshire Dental Service. We were an independent not-for-profit championed by dentists in New Hampshire who were looking for a way to provide for the oral health of consumers around the state through prepaid programs. By 1971, we grew to serve Maine and Vermont as well as New Hampshire, and the tri-state organization took the Northeast Delta Dental name. Our headquarters is in Concord, New Hampshire, and we have sales and marketing offices in Saco, Maine, and Burlington, Vermont.

Since I joined Northeast Delta Dental as CEO in 1995, my team and I have worked to understand who we are and what we do that sets us apart from others. Having an accurate and shared view of our organization is vital to our success because it aligns our thinking and is a valuable part of new-employee onboarding. Because Northeast Delta Dental believes in the power of the Baldrige Excellence Framework, we use its list of descriptive elements in company training materials and here in this book. I realize that many readers may not focus on the details of my business in this section, but I recommend that you study the elements (such as knowing your many stakeholders, your products and services, and your competitors) that make up a complete understanding of a business.

A. Key Stakeholders

All our stakeholders are important to our success, and we work hard to please them and develop lasting and mutually beneficial relationships with them.

Employees

Employees are the people who make an organization work. (Internally at Northeast Delta Dental, we call our employees "employee colleagues" because they work as a collegial team and view each other as colleagues. However, for this book, we will refer to them simply as "employees.") I cannot overstate their importance and value to us before and during the crisis. While they work in several locations doing many jobs, they are all vital to our success. We have grown from a team of 90 when I arrived in 1995 to 232 employees before the crisis hit, with 216 in New Hampshire and sixteen in other states. I'll say more later about how we have worked to support and recognize our employees and have received numerous awards for being such a great place to work.

I could never have accomplished all that I describe in this book without Northeast Delta Dental's incredible leadership team that makes everything this book describes possible. They make our organization run smoothly and well, and I recognize and appreciate their importance to our success.

- Erica Bodwell, Esquire, Former Vice President & General Counsel
- Francis R. Boucher, Senior Vice President, Finance
- Michael D. Bourbeau, Vice President, Information Systems

- Sara M. Brehm, Director Board Relations & Executive Team
- Michel E. Couret, DDS, Chief Dental Officer
- Brian Duffy, Esquire, Vice President and General Counsel
- Joseph V. Errante, DDS, Vice President, Network & Clinical Strategies
- Benantonio Forgione, GBDS, REBC, csONE® COO
- Jodie Hittle, Vice President, Sales & Marketing
- William H. Lambrukos, Senior Vice President, Operations
- Courtney M. Morin, FSA, MAAA, Vice President, Actuarial & Underwriting
- Linda J. Roche, Director, Account Services & Strategic Projects
- Connie M. Roy-Czyzowski, SPHR, SHRM-SCP, CCP, Vice President, Human Resources
- Eugene Shimelfarb, PreViser® CEO
- Kathleen B. Walker, APR, MS, Director, Marketing and Communications

Board Members

A productive and active **Board** is essential to any company's success. This is especially true for Northeast Delta Dental, which operates in three states and has four Boards, one for each state and one overall Board. The 42 members of our Northeast Delta Dental Board of Directors and Trustees support the company's values and govern the enterprise. Board and management alignment are part of our "secret sauce" that was critical to our success during the pandemic.

Our Participating Dentists

For dental insurers, dentists and oral surgeons can choose to participate or not, and those who do are called **participating dentists**. The participating dentists are paid directly by us for the treatments they provide our insured customers and receive other benefits (such as help finding dental supplies). From 957 participating providers when I arrived in 1995, we grew to 1,761 participating providers at the beginning of 2019, a growth of 84%. It's even more impressive when we realize there are about 1,900 dentist practices in our tri-state area, which means about 90% of them participate with us.

Customers

Every organization knows the importance of understanding who its **customers** are and what causes them to be loyal or not. Northeast Delta Dental's customers who purchase our insurance may be either employers of any size and industry (from small country stores to major manufacturers) who buy our insurance as a benefit for their employees, or they may be individuals who buy our insurance for themselves and their families. Initially, we focused on the group insurance business and marketed to those customers business-to-business. In 2010, Congress passed the Affordable Care Act. This meant that individuals needed to buy insurance, which encouraged us to develop and market dental insurance for individual consumers. Both group and individual customers are important to us.

Every policy is in the name of a "subscriber" and may cover family members as well as the subscriber. In 1995, we had about 136,000 subscribers, and this had grown 265% to nearly 500,000 subscribers before the crisis. The number of "covered lives" (including subscribers and family members) more than tripled from about 301,500 in 1995 to 938,000 by the end of 2020.

We have set for ourselves the challenging strategic goal of serving 1 million covered lives. We focus on attracting the people who need our services most: the people who have no dental insurance at all. Of the about 3.2 million people in our tri-state area, we cannot sell to about half of them because they work for organizations such as Walmart that are headquartered outside our territory and are served by other Delta Dental Member Companies. So, our goal of providing healthy smiles to 1 million out of 1.6 million potential customers is ambitious and will require our continued dedication.

Brokers and Benefit Consultants

Insurance **brokers** are go-betweens who sell our insurance products to both small group employers and individual buyers and whose commissions are paid out of the insurance premiums. **Benefit consultants** are independent consultants who advise and are paid directly by large group employers. In 1995, we had 959 brokers/benefit consultants. Today we have 1,279 of them. The increase has resulted primarily from the passage of the Affordable Care Act and our increased sales to individuals.

Communities

All organizations exist in and need to consider their communities. Northeast Delta Dental serves the citizens in the **communities** in our tri-state area even if they are not direct customers because we care about their well-being. The most important element in our mission is the statement that "Everybody Deserves a Healthy Smile," and I cannot overstate how dedicated we are at Northeast Delta Dental to promoting oral health. I recommend a book on the subject by award-winning medical journalist Mary Otto called *Teeth: The Story of Beauty, Inequality, and the Struggle for Oral Health in America*. It vividly portrays the sad reality that poverty and inequality too often prevent people from receiving dental and orthodontic care and force them to live with constant pain and the embarrassment of unsightly teeth.

Because Northeast Delta Dental cares so much, we focus on improving the oral health of our communities, looking beyond our paying customers to everyone in our three states regardless of whether they are insured or not. To reach beyond our paying customers, we established our Northeast Delta Dental Foundation in 1995. Each state contributes financially to the Foundation and relies on it to take a scientific and equitable approach to oral health philanthropy. In addition, all three of our Delta Dental Plans (Delta Dental Plan of Maine, Delta Dental Plan of New Hampshire, and Delta Dental Plan of Vermont) have established a strategic philanthropic framework that provides significant donations and sponsorships to our communities.

We have dentist loan repayment programs and provide scholarships for dental and dental hygiene students because there are not enough dentists or dental hygienists in certain rural areas of our three states. This is part of a typical letter that we receive each year from our endowed scholarship students at Tufts University School of Dental Medicine.

> *Dear Mr. Raffio,*
> *Thank you for the generous scholarship ... I eagerly await the time*
> *when I can return home and work in a rural area in need of oral health care*
> *professionals ... The scholarship has provided additional motivation to return*
> *to Maine to provide quality care, while educating and emphasizing the*
> *importance of oral care to families like mine.*

Both our Foundation and our corporation support oral care for children whose families cannot afford to pay and for veterans whose oral care needs are not met by the Veterans Administration. In 2020, the Foundation and the corporation invested $402,500 in dental education payments and $174,100 in on-site dentistry at Boys and Girls Clubs, schools, and other organizations to bring dentistry to underserved populations.

The Foundation continues to work to identify and eliminate disparities in access to dental health. We know that, as with medical care, communities of color are not well served, and we are determined to make improvements and bring more equity to dental health. While we have worked tirelessly for decades to bring dental care to underserved populations, the Black Lives Matter movement has reinvigorated our mission-sensitive responsibility as a trusted corporate citizen to do even more. To that end, we have developed a strategic initiative to further embed diversity, equity, and inclusion into everything we do as an organization. Our goal is to broaden perspectives among our Board and workforce and to continue putting into practice programs and policies that help mitigate inequities.

Our company also supports many nonprofits with missions unrelated to dental health because we think this is important to help our communities thrive. We support the arts, community service, sports, child care/early learning, and organizations that serve those who are physically challenged. For example, I am an engaged board member of Early Learning New Hampshire, proud to be Chair of the New Hampshire Business Committee for the Arts, which is an excellent intersection of the business and arts communities, and I was Chair of the New Hampshire Symphony Orchestra. In 2020 alone, Northeast Delta Dental invested over $2 million in community nonprofits of all types over and above what we invested in oral health for the under-served.

Finally, donating funds is not the only way we help our communities. Our employees set a notably high standard for volunteering and giving back. Many employees volunteer hundreds of hours of their time and expertise each year. Some provide leadership. For example, in 2020, 42 employees provided 4,332 hours of leadership service to community nonprofits, averaging 103 hours per person. Our Volunteer Involvement Pays (VIP) program gives one day off per year for volunteering through the plan's criteria. We also match employee donations to nonprofits.

Suppliers

Suppliers play an important role in the success of any organization. If suppliers perform well, they help make the organization look good. Conversely, if suppliers perform poorly, they can damage the reputation of an organization.

Northeast Delta Dental has more than 20,000 suppliers. Suppliers include everyone from individuals who care for our plants and stock our vending machines to large organizations that supply strategically important services such as our software and technology platforms or our HIPAA-protected benefits statements for our insureds. Our suppliers break down roughly as follows:

Description	% of Total
Technology support	38%
Claims payment and operational support (clearing houses that send electronic claims from dentists to the correct insurer or that handle the purchase options and payments from individual subscribers)	35%
Building and infrastructure support (electricians, plumbers, security, landscaping, etc.)	8%
Marketing	7%
Miscellaneous (including insurance, financial, and product partners)	12%

In particular, there are 50 critical vendor/supplier partners without whom we could not operate optimally. These key partners are reviewed annually with a sophisticated compliance checklist, following a Baldrige framework. We believe, as

Professor Ron Adner once said, that we are only as strong as our weakest partner. So, we work hard to help our suppliers maintain their quality. For instance, we use tools such as the Service Organization Control (SOC) report, which evaluates the risks and controls of an organization, to manage our technology partners. For those interested in learning more about the importance of the interdependence of customer companies and suppliers, I recommend Rod Adner's book, *The Wide Lens: A New Strategy for Innovation*.

B. Environment and Products

Regulatory Environment

Every organization must be responsive to its regulatory environment. Northeast Delta Dental is regulated by the insurance commissioners in our three states, and we are proud to be a member of the national Delta Dental Plans Association (DDPA). Today, DDPA is comprised of a network of 39 independent Delta Dental Member Companies operating in all 50 states, Puerto Rico, and other U.S. territories. All Delta Dental Member Companies share a mission to put a healthier, happier smile on every American's face by providing greater access to oral health care. Nationally, DDPA covers more than 83 million Americans, and together we provide coverage to more Americans than any other dental insurance company.

Products and Services

Products and services are crucial to all organizations. If they are well designed and produced, they attract customers, and they can gain or lose customers depending on how well they fulfill customer needs.

When Northeast Delta Dental began, it focused entirely on providing one product: dental insurance. Over time, we have grown our business substantially by adding new products and services.

Our first new product, begun in 2009, was our vision insurance, **DeltaVision®**, initially offered in New Hampshire and Maine and, more recently, in Vermont. We added it because many group customers asked us to offer additional insurance products. We began with vision because vision care and dental care practices are similar in size and structure, and insurance regulations for both are similar.

A second offering is **csONE®**, our general insurance agency, which enables us to sell our own products as well as other firms' life insurance and auxiliary lines to our business clients. We acquired csONE® because many of our group customers and benefits consultants said they preferred to deal with a single insurance agency. csONE® is governed by Northeast Delta Dental's Subsidiary Board and has its own dedicated employees. It turned out, during the pandemic crisis, that having csONE® was an important benefit to many subscribers because it allowed us to identify and offer continuing dental insurance to subscribers who were laid off by their employers. This was possible because the Consolidated Omnibus Budget Reconciliation Act (COBRA) gives workers and their families who lose their health benefits the right to choose to continue group health benefits provided by their group health plan.

A third new service is **PreViser**®, a software product that we give to our dentists because it supports our mission of better oral health for all. One key element of PreViser® is a software assessment tool that we call Health *through* Oral Wellness®, or HOW®. HOW® lets dentists determine, graph, and track the optimum number of visits per year for each individual patient. While some patients only need two visits a year, close to 50% of patients require three or more cleanings and other procedures. HOW® is a win/win/win tool because it allows dentists to provide more services per year when warranted, improves the dental health of many subscribers, and earns Northeast Delta Dental goodwill and loyalty from dentists and subscribers. HOW® is so popular that it is being used by other Delta Dental Member Companies and their dentists. PreViser® is governed by Northeast Delta Dental's Subsidiary Board and has its own dedicated employees.

PreViser® Proven to Prevent Disease and Save Money

    PreViser®, a personalized approach to oral healthcare, has been proven to reduce oral care costs and help prevent many serious medical illnesses. The online PreViser® risk assessment tool evaluates patients' oral care needs based on their risk of gum disease or periodontitis. Gum disease has been linked to stroke, heart disease, and diabetes, so preventing gum disease with more frequent dental visits is an excellent investment.

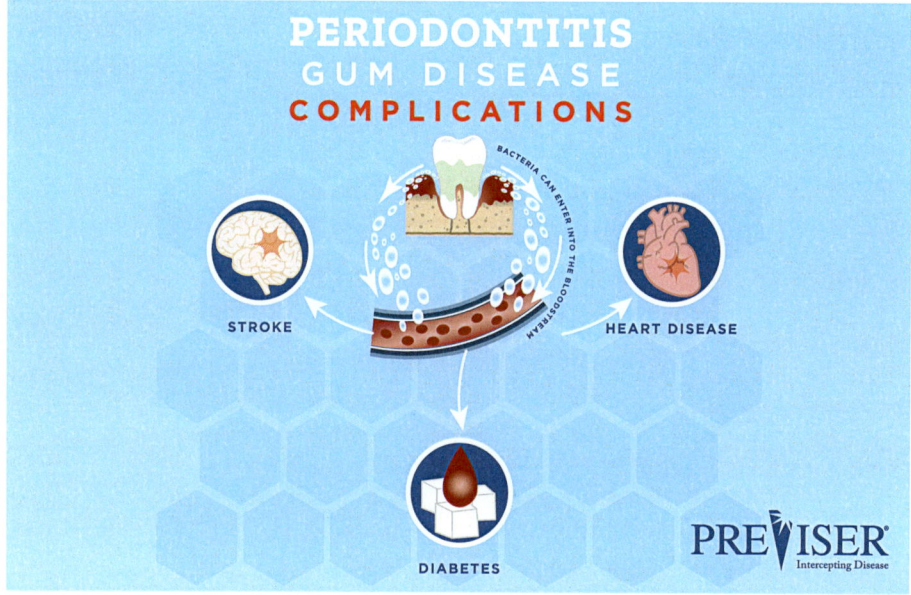

    Since 2015, PreViser's® risk-based personalized dental benefits analysis has helped major dental insurance companies, over two million of their plan members, and their employers save millions of dollars in preventable oral and medical illnesses and also prevent needless patient suffering and time loss. PreViser® is the only assessment platform scientifically validated to predict the risk and cost of costly gum disease and the resulting savings in preventable oral surgery, prosthodontics, and adjunctive services.

    While the cost of preventive dental care was 14% higher for groups with PreViser® in the five years between 2015 and 2020, the cost of oral surgery was 21% lower, the cost of prosthodontics was 11% lower, and the cost of other adjunctive dental services was 14% lower.

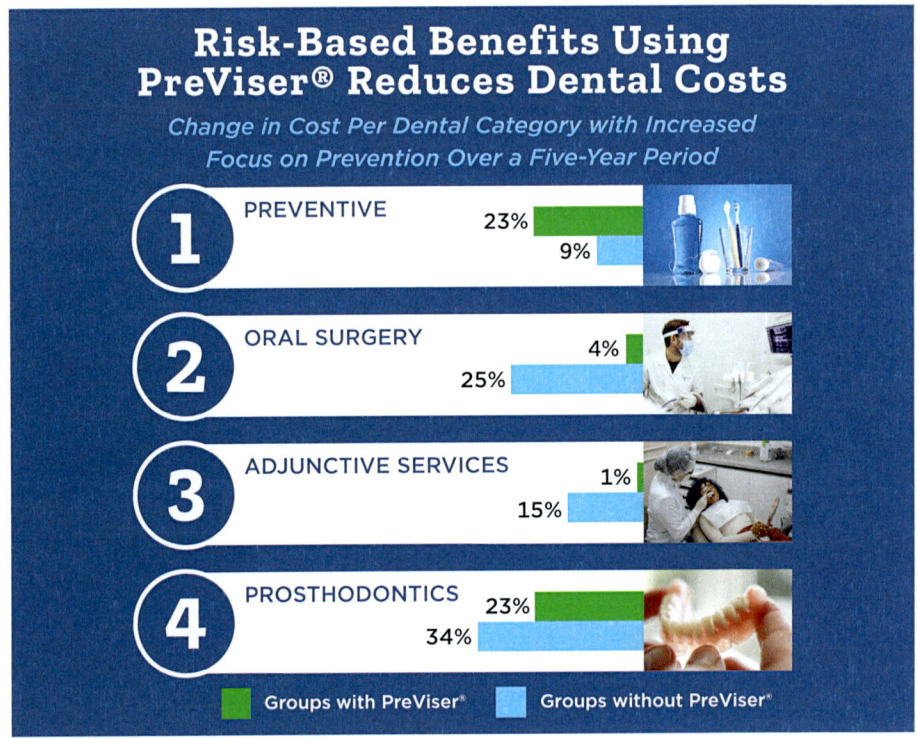

C. Competitive Situation

Every organization faces competition, and the most successful organizations know that they have to work hard and stay alert to outperform their competitors.

Northeast Delta Dental has many competitors and respects them all. Many commercial insurers such as Cigna or Anthem offer dental as well as integrated health insurance. In contrast, Northeast Delta Dental cannot offer a health insurance product. However, while these competitors are bigger and broader than we are, we almost never lose business to them because our customers know and appreciate our quality, our customer service, our extensive network of dentists, and our HOW® program powered by PreViser®. As a result, we keep 98% of our group customers year after year, well above the Delta Dental system average of 92% and the 87% average for the national dental insurance industry.

One of our differentiators in the insurance industry is our commitment to continuous quality improvement. I introduced the principles of the Malcolm Baldrige

National Quality Award to our senior executives when I arrived in 1995, and many of our managers and non-managers took the training to be Baldrige examiners at the national or state levels and continue to use its principles today. This aligned our thinking about good management and still binds us today. Bill Lambrukos (Senior Vice President, Operations), Linda Roche (Director, Account Services & Strategic Projects), and Connie Roy-Czyzowski (Vice President, Human Resources) on our Northeast Delta Dental leadership team today took this training and use its principles.

I continue to deepen Northeast Delta Dental's understanding and appreciation of the most effective quality standards. We have made and will continue to make improvements in all aspects of our business policies and operations. I am an incorporator and Chair of the Board of the ExcellenceNorth Alliance (formerly Granite State Quality Council), the Baldrige organization serving Maine, New Hampshire, and Vermont. Several of our employees provide leadership to the organization, and we host many of its events.

Northeast Delta Dental is known for partnering with other organizations to find lasting oral health solutions and for our dedication to encouraging people to view oral health as a vital component of overall health. To that end, we convene forums to encourage physicians and dentists to find ways to work together to benefit their patients. With more than a half century of experience developing innovative programs for dental benefits administration, our leadership team has earned a reputation for its expertise in the dental insurance industry.

Northeast Delta Dental has won numerous awards for its role in the community, including:

- Business of the Year (Insurance Category) by *Business NH Magazine* and the NH Association of Chamber of Commerce Executives – 1997, 2001, and 2021
- Concord Coalition to End Homelessness Pillar of Support – 2021
- Recognition for Excellence from Workgroup for Electronic Interchange – 2018
- Above and Beyond Award from Business and Industry Association of NH – 2014
- New England Higher Education Excellence Award – 2013
- USA Track and Field Mountain Ultra Trail Council Contributor of the year – 2012

- New Hampshire Partners in Education – 2011
- Key Business Partner from Tesia Clearinghouse – 2010
- Computerworld Laureate Award – 2009
- Presidents' Community Partners Award – 2009
- National Alliance on Mental Illness Community Leadership Award – 2007
- Honoree by *Computerworld* for Best Practices in Storage Innovation – 2007
- Vendor of the Year from NY Motor Transport Association – 2003
- New Hampshire Business Committee for the Arts Business Award – 2002
- Granite State Quality Achievement Award – 2000

Having this kind of clear and written understanding of how your organization operates and whom it serves ensures that your managers do not overlook something vital when reacting to a crisis.

Karen Metz, Sales Executive: The joy of working from home

3. Make Serving Your Customers a Top Priority

When I consider my experiences with many firms where I'm a customer, such as internet or phone providers, their employees often make me feel like a nuisance during our interactions. In contrast, at Northeast Delta Dental, we know we exist for our customers. We recognize that they are our reason for being, so we have a more determined drive to please customers than most other firms.

There are 39 other Delta Dental Member Companies across the country, and Northeast Delta Dental has the highest customer retention rate of them all: around 98% of our group customers typically renew with us each year. We work hard to earn their loyalty.

To emphasize our commitment to quality, Northeast Delta Dental introduced our service guarantee program in 1996, a year after I became President & CEO. With the guidance and support of a guarantee team headed by Linda Roche (then Director of Marketing and now Director of Account Services & Strategic Projects), we researched and introduced our **Guarantee Of Service Excellence**[SM] (GOSE[SM]), which reinforces our commitment to customers by giving refunds when we fail to perform up to our high standards. It was the first such program in Northern New England; and it benefits us, in addition to our customers, because it keeps us reevaluating and improving every aspect of our business, with the customers in mind. GOSE[SM], as described in the book *Relentless* by John Tschohl, has strengthened our brand, and has built our reputation for excellent customer service and quality performance.

Let me give a personal example of how incredibly well our people interact with customers. We had a frontline receptionist, Suzanne Wason, who sat in the entrance lobby at headquarters and who also answered all calls that came to the general phone line and were not routed to others. She posted the names of each day's visitors on an old-fashioned bulletin board behind her desk because she knew people liked being recognized. She learned callers' voices and could converse with them as individuals. And, of course, she knew just where to direct all callers. I can't tell you how often I got calls and notes praising her. Suzanne has recently retired and is enjoying her next chapter in life. Before her last day, which was a happy one for Suzanne but a sad one for Northeast Delta Dental, in the true Baldrige fashion, she trained not two but three receptionists who have taken up the baton. I now receive rave review notes about the three employees trained by Suzanne. And I sleep well at night knowing that all our customer service representatives, marketers, and others are equally skilled.

An operational example of how well we serve our customers has been the work led by Senior Vice President, Operations, William Lambrukos. He has served Northeast Delta Dental for 45 years and has been a staunch advocate of continuous improvement and performance excellence. He and his team are constantly working to improve our work processes, such as call answering, to make them quicker and better for customers. They have done such great work that customers who call in reach a live service representative in an average of under 30 seconds and have nearly 100% of their calls resolved on first contact. It's another reason I sleep well at night.

It's impossible to overstate the importance of making customers a top priority. Firms that compete only on price can always be undercut. Those that compete on quality always win in the long run because that's the way to earn customer loyalty. Having earned and built a loyal customer base into our foundation was a tremendous asset to Northeast Delta Dental when the COVID-19 crisis struck.

4. Create a High-Functioning Board Using Best Governance Practices

Northeast Delta Dental operates in three states and has four Boards, one for each state and one overall Northeast Delta Dental Board. Their membership is approximately 50% dental professionals and 50% business or community leaders. The Maine and New Hampshire Boards each have 15 Directors, while the Vermont Board has 12 Trustees, making a total of 42 Board members in the tri-state area. Sara Brehm, Director of Board Relations & Executive Team on Northeast Delta Dental's leadership team, does a Herculean job ensuring that our governance policies and practices meet all state requirements while maintaining excellent communications with our various Boards.

Because the tri-state Northeast Delta Dental Boards have so many members, we created four-member to five-member Executive Committees (ECs) for each state. These state-specific ECs meet in between the quarterly full Board meetings and are empowered to authorize actions that will be approved later by the whole Board. As you can imagine, the existence of the ECs had a huge and positive impact on our ability to react quickly when the pandemic hit.

We also have two other Boards that should be mentioned:
- Northeast Delta Dental Foundation Board – governing our nonprofit charitable organization
- Northeast Delta Dental Subsidiary Board – governing our csONE® and PreViser® product lines of business

At Northeast Delta Dental, we committed to state-of-the-art corporate governance before it was the popular thing to do. Although we are not technically subject to the provisions of Sarbanes-Oxley because we are not a publicly-traded company, we believe in the spirit and purpose of this accountability act and have tailored many of our internal financial control policies and procedures and Board-level reviews to its superior standards. Other best practices examples include our 1) Board skills recruitment, 2) Board member code of conduct, 3) annual evaluations of Board members, 4) annual Board evaluation of the CEO, 5) Board member training, and 6) anticipating needed innovations and future risks.

Potential new Board members are all interviewed and vetted by the Corporate Governance Committees in Maine and Vermont and the External Nominating Committee in New Hampshire before being recommended to the full Board. We know that we need a mixture of dental professionals and business or community leaders with impeccable reputations, but we also know that we need certain skills on our Boards. These skill sets may change over time, making it important to think strategically about the skills and who may possess them. For example, we know that cybersecurity is vital to Northeast Delta Dental because almost all, if not all, of our daily work rests on our technology infrastructure and databases. So, during the past few years, several of our new Board members were recruited for their experience with state-of-the-art cybersecurity practices.

We also know that Diversity, Equity, and Inclusion (DEI) are vital to Northeast Delta Dental. DEI is an overarching goal of the company and key to addressing oral health disparities, so Northeast Delta Dental is authentically committed to DEI and to bringing diversity to our Board. Nearly 50% of our 42-member tri-state Board are women, and about 20% are black, indigenous, or people of color (BIPOC). We were committed to diversity long before the Black Lives Matter movement brought this issue to the forefront, and we currently have a tri-state Board DEI committee that is working to address oral health disparities among ethnic groups in our states. It also works in concert with other Board committees to support recruiting more minority Board members. As for our top leadership, nearly 40% are women, and we expect more diversity in our top leadership as retirements happen. Northeast Delta Dental's long-term support of the Black New England Conference and engagement with other organizations that support DEI initiatives sets the tone and has authentically connected us with the BIPOC community. (See page 135 in the Communications Appendix.)

All Board members, new and veteran, must read and sign the Northeast Delta Dental Code of Conduct every year. Peer evaluations, self-evaluations, meeting attendance and preparation, and other metrics of Board member performance from the Corporate Directors/Trustees Code of Conduct are done annually to ensure optimal Board performance and optimal Board room dynamics. Each Board member receives her or his performance metrics juxtaposed to the corporate norm, and Board members are encouraged to talk with the Board Chair or the Chair of the Governance Committee should there be any questions on the results. These evaluations are used by the Governance Committee/External Nominating Committee to determine whether a Board member should continue to serve a second or third term. This process keeps our Board members active, fresh, and committed.

The Board does a formal, detailed evaluation of me as the CEO every year. Every Board member provides input to my annual CEO Evaluation, as does the senior team via a confidential 180-degree review process. I am evaluated on my leadership in terms of these criteria:
1. Fostering innovation and agility
2. Promoting diversity
3. Committing to our mission, vision, and values
4. Focusing on our priorities
5. Being open to professional development and continuous improvement

In addition, I am evaluated on my ability to achieve "Level 5 Leadership" status as identified by Jim Collins in his book, *Good to Great*. Level 5 refers to the highest level in a hierarchy of executive capabilities identified by the research of Jim Collins and his team. Level 5 Leadership includes personal humility, producing sustained results, concern for the company's success rather than personal recognition or wealth, setting up successors for success, and taking responsibility when things go poorly while attributing success to others.

Finally, the Board reviews our succession plans each year to be sure Northeast Delta Dental will be able to carry on if top executives are lost for some reason.

In 1997, we began formal training for all Board members. For new Board members, we provide a one-day intensive training program in our Concord, New Hampshire, headquarters to meet our staff and learn about our governance practices. We also send Board members to a training program in Chicago by the National Association of Corporate Directors. Experienced Board members are sent to a two-and-a-half-day training program put on by the Harvard Business

School. So far, nearly 70 Board members have participated in the course, "Making Corporate Boards More Effective." One of the best outcomes of this training is that we ask all participants to write up what they have learned and suggest how Northeast Delta Dental could improve its governance practices. We then use their suggestions to help us remain state of the art. As one recent attendee of the training wrote, "It was heartening to see that Northeast Delta Dental corporate governance follows nearly all best practices presented. It was a challenge to find [ways of how] we may continue the improvement of our Board operations."

Good governance calls for the Boards to review all financials, review and approve the budgets, set CEO compensation and contract terms, and guide and approve strategic plans, including all new business ventures. The Boards' Finance/Audit Committees and the tri-state Compensation and Compliance Committee take the lead on this with the input and support of the full Boards. Our Boards go beyond that by participating in off-site strategic planning days that allow us to address risks and risk management, emerging technologies, succession plans, and innovations to ensure Northeast Delta Dental and its three state groups are making progress toward our strategic goals.

In short, we have established clear procedures for securing and ensuring high-quality Board input and review through our governance practices. These practices have developed strong mutual trust between Northeast Delta Dental management and our Board members. And, in between our quarterly Board meetings, we have the Executive Committees review and approve actions as needed.

As you can imagine, recruiting and nurturing high-functioning and dedicated Board members was critical for Northeast Delta Dental's success during the COVID-19 crisis. Some business leaders believe they are managed by their boards, but it is equally important for a CEO to help develop a high-functioning board.

5. Establish Trusting Relationships with Legislators and Regulators

In addition to the strong relationships we develop with our Board members, we have also worked to establish trusting relationships with our legislators and regulators in Maine, New Hampshire, and Vermont for over 20 years. We hold annual receptions in each state capitol to get to know and thank them for their service without asking them for anything in return. Taking this long view has proven helpful, as we observed when Northeast Delta Dental was allowed to be included in state-based exchanges for marketing dental insurance to individuals, not just HR managers, in accordance with the Affordable Care Act.

For the regulators, other top Northeast Delta Dental executives (such as our former General Counsel Erica Bodwell and our current General Counsel Brian Duffy) and I also meet annually with the heads of insurance in each state. We remind them who we are and what we are doing for their states, and we ask what their issues are. These dialogs help ensure they are ready to trust us when their support is needed.

As you will read in the next section of this book, we were able to secure needed approvals to respond to the COVID-19 crisis very quickly because of the relationships we established with the legislators and regulators. We were able to accomplish this because we got to know and trust each other over the years.

6. Create a Robust Strategic Planning Process and Goals

It is vital to have a robust planning process and clear strategic plans (both long-term and annual) to guide and align an organization and set the tone and plans for the coming years.

When I arrived as CEO in 1995, I found that our governing Boards were accustomed to conducting strategic planning. Over time, our strategic plan goals have evolved to focus on three target areas.

Our Main Strategic Goals

Net Growth. Our goal is to have 1 million customers (covered lives) out of a total eligible tri-state population of about 1.6 million. This is over 60% of those eligible and is ambitious but motivating.

Profitability. As a not-for-profit organization, our goal is not to make huge profits but to have a balanced budget and to be able to add enough to our reserves to act as a cushion in times of crisis and to allow us to pursue our strategic objectives.

Administrative Cost. Although about 90% of our costs are what we pay our dentists, we have a responsibility to keep our administrative costs to about 10% of revenue, which we have accomplished successfully over time.

Although the Boards participated in strategic planning when I arrived, I recognized that the process needed improvement. In 1995, the Boards of each of our three states held separate retreats to do their planning. This was inefficient and ineffective. It meant that, if one state decided to do something new, I then had to work with the other states to get them to accept the idea. Also, three small organizations did not have the same clout, resources, and reserves as the larger combined Northeast Delta Dental. The solution was to get the three separate legal entities to act together as a nimble and efficient mid-sized entity.

So, the first change we made to our strategic planning process was to get the three state Boards to agree to joint strategic planning. With 42 Board members, a few lawyers, and over two dozen Northeast Delta Dental executives attending the combined planning retreat, this was definitely a challenge and still is. We do a great deal of preparation beforehand to organize the process and to ensure everyone is prepared and comfortable. We worked hard in the beginning to intersperse people from the three states and to mix the dentists with the non-dentists. The first couple of years, it was easy to see who was from which state and occupation, but I'm delighted to say that today it is difficult to tell people apart as everyone focuses on our shared vision and goals. I would challenge any observer to successfully guess which Board member is a dentist or non-dentist and what state the Board member represents.

A second change we made to our strategic planning process was its timing. We used to hold our planning retreats in the fall (a lovely time in New England), but by the time we worked on the retreat outcomes and wrote the strategic plan, there was no time to produce an annual budget that reflected the strategic goals. With our annual fiscal year running with the calendar year (January through December), we realized that we needed to hold our planning retreats at least six months (rather than three) before the beginning of the budget cycle. So, now we hold our retreats in May or June, which gives us time to assemble the plan details and budget to support the plan.

A third improvement we made was to make sure all our three primary strategic goals (net growth, profitability, and administrative costs) were translated into what the business community calls SMART goals. That stands for:

Strategic
Measurable
Achievable
Realistic
Time Based

We have found that having clear, measurable targets with time horizons for our organization keeps us on track. Also, the Board discusses progress on the SMART goals and progress on our strategic goals at each Board meeting and at monthly chair leadership teleconferences.

A fourth improvement we made was to offer Team Bonuses to employees for achieving their SMART goals. We translate all goals into team or department goals so that everyone can see a direct line of sight from their work to the overall organization's success. At first, some departments said they didn't recognize these connections. For instance, Marketing wondered how they affected operating costs. But then they realized that they minimized operations time and cost by marketing and selling dental plan designs that were as uncomplicated and as similar as possible. Similarly, Customer Service saw that by spending time with customers on the phone, they could not only solve concerns but prevent future problems. Claims realized that speedy and accurate claims processing avoided problems and repeat work. Operations, with their superlative service, assisted the Marketing team in boosting the renewals that are critical in the group insurance business. With Team Bonus tracking, everyone had a better understanding of their roles in retaining satisfied customers.

We put aside about $1 million a year for our overall Team Bonus. If we achieve our target measures, we pay out the whole $1 million. If we achieve 75% of our measures, then we pay out $750,000, and so on. We feel this is money very well invested because it keeps everyone throughout the organization focused and aware of the importance of their performance.

So, why are these improvements to our strategic planning process important during a crisis? Combining the three state Board plans into a single Northeast Delta Dental plan is important because it aligns tri-state goals and resources and unites us in agreeing on what's important. Retiming the planning retreat is essential because it allows us to set a financial budget each year that reflects our strategic priorities. And setting SMART goals and bonuses is important because it keeps our progress toward our strategic goals visible and motivational to everyone from Board members to all employees.

I stress the work we have done on improving our strategic planning process because all these changes made it much easier for us to plan how to act during the pandemic.

7. Plan Ahead for a Crisis — Build Resiliency

Our annual strategic plans focused on the future, but they typically did this by assuming business would carry on as usual, for the most part. On the other hand, we realized that disasters could occur at any time and that we needed to be prepared for them. So, in 2016, we contracted with Advizex, a firm that specializes in disaster planning, to help us develop our disaster recovery plan.

This plan covered all types of disasters, including natural (weather) disasters; fires, bombs, and explosions; power and equipment failures; nuclear, biological, and chemical accidents; intruders; suspicious packages; and (at the end of the list) pandemics. I had read about the flu of 1918 in John Barry's best-selling book *The Great Influenza: The Story of the Deadliest Pandemic in History*, and knew that pandemics were always possible, though if you had asked me about the odds of a pandemic hitting us, I would have said, "Very low."

Our first plan of action was how to evacuate our offices in case the disaster threatened our two Concord, New Hampshire, headquarters' buildings (Delta One and Delta Two) or other offices. After that, we had specific component plans that could be combined and put into action as appropriate for each disaster type. The components had four basic elements:

1. Incident Detection, Notification, and Evacuation

2. Initial Assessment by the Incident Recovery Team (IRT) – Specific employees were identified as the IRT members. For instance, we had a Pandemic Recovery Team already assigned before the COVID-19 crisis struck.)

3. Recovery Location and Recovery of Business Operations – Our Pandemic Team began to meet virtually every Thursday by Webex, beginning on March 12, to guide the recovery. We primarily used Webex early in the pandemic for security reasons; but then, later, Zoom improved its security platform, and we used both Webex and Zoom.

4. Business Return to Site and Normal Operations

We learned several important things during our disaster planning. First, this had to be a living document. We had to keep the members of our Incident Recovery Teams up-to-date and fully trained for their roles. We had to periodically update the plan to reflect changes in our operations or vulnerabilities. And we had to periodically hold simulations to test the plans.

Second, we learned that each department had to have its own disaster recovery plan. Using our Customer Service group as an example, their plan revealed their dependence on technology for all operations (handling customer inquiries and claims processing) and their interconnection with all other departments. Their plan laid out the need to quickly find secure replacement technologies and the timelines needed to get them back up and running. For instance, if we had to evacuate our offices, then people would have to work from home; and this would require a new call handling system to distribute the calls to many sites. Another example is from our External Affairs group, which changed its media support firm to have one that was available 24/7. This change seemed small but turned out to have a huge impact during the pandemic.

When each department looked at the impact of each type of disaster on its business, we realized that we were very vulnerable if we didn't move away from paper-based processes to more secure electronic processes. Under the guidance of Mike Bourbeau, our Vice President of Information Systems, we determined we needed to have robust electronic ways to communicate with our entire employee group and with customers and dentists.

In our round of strategic planning for FY 2019, this led us to plan and budget for a substantial technology upgrade to our phone system. We recognized that our automatic call distribution system needed to support those representatives working from home as well as those in the office. This automated call answering system is crucial because it distributes calls in order of receipt, measures the speed of answering and other essential quality indicators, and supports performance standards that our customers and the Delta Dental Plans Association require.

Equally important, Mike and his team emphasized that the new system had to be secure from cyber threats, especially since any representatives working from home would not have the usual firewalls all our in-office devices have.

We ordered the new system to be installed in the fall of 2020, six months too late for the COVID-19 pandemic response. Even so, our disaster recovery plan readied us to respond. We had 20 of our customer service reps come into the office in person. Since there were only 20 of them instead of the usual 100 people in that space, we could physically distance them, and there were no safety issues. When the new phone system was working in October 2020, we made a seamless switchover. This enabled our customer service representatives and others to work safely, quickly, and efficiently from home.

Another effort that emerged from our disaster recovery planning was that we purchased 500 high-quality blue surgical masks for our staff to use during a pandemic. How wise we were. More on this later.

All of these plans and actions added to what many experts call our "resiliency." A highly-respected and influential organization (the Baldrige Performance Excellence Program) added the concept of resiliency to its 2021-2022 excellence framework. It defines resiliency as:

1. Planning for and recovering from disasters or crises
2. Protecting and enhancing stakeholder (customer, employee, society) well-being, financial performance, and organizational productivity

Robert Fangmeyer, the Director of the Baldrige Performance Excellence Program, describes resiliency as more than just bouncing back to the status quo but bouncing forward to be even better than you were before the crisis. I am so pleased that Northeast Delta Dental undertook our disaster recovery planning when we did because, as you will see, it helped us be resilient during the COVID crisis.

8. Build a Strong Infrastructure

The most important elements of our infrastructure are our employees, our robust technology, and our work processes; and my leadership team and I have worked hard to support and strengthen them all.

Our exceptional employees make us unique. They delight our customers, dentists, and other stakeholders. They are the heart of Northeast Delta Dental, and my role as CEO is to support them.

In that regard, possibly my most important role is mentoring and role modeling for our emerging young leaders. I encourage them to go out into the community, to meet other future leaders, to help nonprofits, and to get out of their comfort zones and take leadership skills training (such as Hoffman-Haas). I especially like it when our employees take Toastmasters training, because it prepares them to be leaders who can communicate and speak effectively in public.

Occasionally some of our up-and-coming employees get hired away for great jobs. I'm not disappointed when this happens but see it as a beautiful thing. We celebrate what we call their "outside promotions," and my colleagues and I are happy that we had the benefit of their great work for the years they were with us. Another benefit is that many of them recommend Northeast Delta Dental to their new employers!

When I arrived at Northeast Delta Dental and wanted to increase employee engagement, we focused on bringing our benefits and pay up to par. Next, we provided Baldrige performance excellence training and worked to empower and recognize employees for their contributions. In recent years, we have invested in mindfulness training and skills development for all our employees who want to participate. Our mindfulness effort provides time at work for meditation and teaches the importance of unitasking — not multitasking, which slows work and affects accuracy. For those interested in learning more about mindfulness, I've written a book with Dr. Annabel Beerel that describes what we have done. (Please see the list of references at the end of this book.)

Our Vice President, Human Resources, Connie Roy-Czyzowski, has been the architect of most of our employment practices. From day one, I recognized the need for an engaged workforce if we were going to be great. Hiring Connie in 1997 to report directly to me was the perfect way to elevate and show the importance of a self-actualizing workforce to the success of our company. She has taken the human side of our enterprise to the nth degree.

Our investment in our employees has received numerous awards such as:
- One of the Best Companies to Work for in New Hampshire – 1998, 1999, 2000, 2001, 2002, 2016, 2017, 2018, 2019, 2020, and Hall of Fame in 2003, 2004, and 2021
- Fit-Friendly Worksite – 2015
- When Work Works Award – 2010, 2012, 2014
- Alfred P. Sloan Award for Business Excellence in Workplace Flexibility – 2010, 2012
- *New Hampshire Business Review's* Health Innovator Award – 2011
- Psychologically Healthy Workplace Award – 2009, 2011
- American Psychological Association Best Practice Honors – 2010
- Winning Workplaces Hall of Fame – 2009

Perhaps the statistic that says the most about how we invest in and support our employees is our low turnover rate. Our turnover rate before the pandemic in 2019 was under 14%, which compared very favorably to a national turnover rate of nearly 23%.

Around the late 1990s or early 2000s, our strategy called for making a major investment in our information systems software and hardware. Up to that point, we paid an external company with a mainframe to process all our claims payments, but they charged us $1 per claim. We saw that the larger and more successful we grew, the more we had to spend for claims processing. So, in 2003-2004, we invested many millions to bring claims processing in-house. It was huge for us, not only in cost but in the chance for things to go wrong as we made the transition. Fortunately, with good planning and dedication from everyone, it worked out very well. The administrative cost per claim is now less than thirty cents and keeps getting lower the more claims we process. Also, because of our investment in interactive voice recognition (IVR) call technology and our web pages, just one of our great call service reps can handle over 28,000 subscribers a year in 2021 with the same or better average speed of answer as in 2002 (when each rep handled just 16,000 subscribers).

As I mentioned earlier, we learned from our disaster recovery planning that our phone systems needed to be updated, and we budgeted for this. While the system wasn't installed until the fall of 2020, we were still ahead of the game when it was available. If we had tried to plan and order the system during the pandemic, I'm certain the result would have been much slower and probably not implemented as smoothly.

A Board tri-state Technology Committee helps steer our technology and cybersecurity investments and plans based on managerial recommendations. The Board Technology Committee is populated by Board members recruited for their expertise in this field.

One of the Baldrige business management principles we strive for is developing efficient and effective work processes that accomplish what is needed with minimal costs and errors. Under the guidance of our Senior Vice President, Operations, Bill Lambrukos, we have created work processes that are quick and accurate and meet or exceed customer needs; we continue to monitor and improve these processes.

In 2010, when the Affordable Care Act steered us to focus on selling direct to consumers, we also had to adopt different ways of marketing, processing benefits, and answering customer service calls. In addition, each state has its own insurance exchange for consumers, so we had to invest millions to connect to those exchanges and operate within them. We accomplished this with our private exchange tool, **DeltaDentalCoversMe.com**, which was named and built by a handful of Delta Dental Member Companies with Delta Dental of Wisconsin in the lead. Our Vice President of Sales & Marketing, Jodie Hittle, and his team implemented this DeltaDentalCoversMe.com tool for Northeast Delta Dental. It is so easy to use that consumers typically can sign up for Northeast Delta Dental insurance in less than a minute.

Our investments in our top-notch employees and our technological and operational adaptability have resulted in great advantages for us. During the crisis, this investment meant we already knew how to develop innovative and robust work processes in a hurry. Thanks to the leadership of Frank Boucher, Senior Vice President of Finance and CFO, we have built and maintain Northeast Delta Dental's financial reserves while investing in our people and technology. These investments have also yielded excellent financial returns.

9. Be a Servant Leader and Communicate, Communicate, Communicate

When I started my career in my early twenties at John Hancock Mutual Life Insurance Company in Boston, I saw that one of my managers was aloof and authoritarian, while another was positive and caring and led by example. You could say that they exemplified what Douglas McGregor wrote about in 1960 in *The Human Side of Enterprise*, where he talked about Theory X managers (authoritarian) and Theory Y managers (collaborative). I always felt more motivated to work hard for my caring manager than my aloof manager, and this has been the impetus for my own style as a leader for the past forty years. I believe that people will jump through hoops for managers who give them clear direction and support. They will want to do more than what their jobs require if led properly.

I describe my leadership style and that of my leadership team as "servant leadership." The term was coined by Robert Greenleaf of The Greenleaf Center for Servant Leadership in his book, *The Power of Servant Leadership* (1998), and I still refer from time to time to my much-thumbed copy, along with the other seminal work on servant leadership, *Leadership Is an Art*, by Max De Pree, also much dog-eared. Servant leaders put serving others (including employees, customers, and community) first. To me, this relies on communicating honestly and fully, setting clear direction, and providing the training, resources, and empowerment people need to do their jobs to the best of their abilities.

Communication is a big part of being a servant leader. I communicate to define our vision for our employees and to share with them the facts of our business — our reality. Because I communicate with full disclosure and transparency, the few times when I've had to deliver difficult news, my people were able to accept the situation much better than if I had been vague or had not prepared them for the situation.

> "Servant leaders put serving others (including employees, customers, and community) first."

In 1995 when I arrived, before email became widely used, I actively communicated with people. For employees, this meant having personal meetings, doing walk-arounds, and getting to know about their lives and families and concerns. I kept a notebook of key staff news because I wanted to pay attention and make everyone feel heard. Now, of course, we live in a virtual communication world, but the same principles apply. I listen because I care, and I share news honestly in order to build trust. Because we are what I think of as the ideal size organization for communication (around 200 people), it is easier for me than for a CEO of a huge company to communicate with and know everyone.

With the help of Kathleen Walker, our Director of Marketing & Communications, and her team, I use every method at my disposal to keep employees informed of important developments at Northeast Delta Dental.

After each quarterly Northeast Delta Dental Board meeting, I send emails to everyone explaining important data, strategies, and Board decisions.

I send out emails whenever there is good news (like a big new account) or a major event that affects us (like the passage of the Affordable Care Act or installing new phone systems).

Before the pandemic, we held quarterly All Employee Meetings in the Concord headquarters and encouraged the ten marketing/sales people working in our Maine and Vermont offices to attend in person. Also, I periodically visited the Maine and Vermont offices and did regular walk-arounds in New Hampshire.

Since the pandemic, our All Employee Meetings are held virtually each month. And, I continue to contribute to our monthly newsletter, *Team Power*, which combines fun human-interest stories with strategic and business updates. (See *Team Power* samples on pages 61 and 139.)

A final thought on our communications is that I actively listen and seek input as well as talking or sharing what's on my mind. The All Employee Meetings and my frequent walking through the offices are useful for this. We also participate in a New Hampshire Best Company employee engagement survey (similar to an employee climate survey) each year, so we have very specific metrics on the human side of the enterprise. The other companies that take the survey also are New Hampshire companies that enter the competition. In other words, we are comparing ourselves to highly competitive firms.

The table below summarizes the results of just a few of the 14 survey metrics for the past five years (2016-2020). The scores can range from 0-100%, and the table shows our five-year average ratings and our comparisons to norms. While we are proud that we perform well and above norm on all 14 survey metrics, as you can see, we perform especially well on the Communication dimension.

Survey Metric	Northeast Delta Dental Avg. Score 2016-20	Amt. Northeast Delta Dental Scores Above Norm
Highly engaged	80%	+18%
It starts at the top	86%	+17%
Overall (across all metrics)	86%	+13%
Communication	89%	+16%

I've been proud to receive numerous awards for leadership. Some that stand out for me are:
- Baldrige Foundation Award for Leadership Excellence in Healthcare Award – 2020

- Easterseals NH–David P. Goodwin Lifetime Commitment Award – 2020
- The New Hampshire 200 – in 2019
- City Year NH Lifetime of Service Award – 2014
- Granite State Award – 2011
- Business Leader of the Decade – 2010
- Doctor of Humane Letters from New England College – 2010
- Outstanding Citizen of the Year Award – 2009
- Community Leadership Award – 2006
- NH Business Committee for the Arts Business Leader Award – 2005
- Best Bosses (a national joint award from Winning Workplaces and *Fortune Small Business* magazine) – 2005
- The Patrick Jackson Award for Distinguished Service to PRSA – 2004

Bottom Line: I believe servant leadership and a focus on communication are the ideal ways to build trust with employees and to motivate, even inspire, them to perform at their best in good times and in times of crisis.

10. Insist on Best Management Practices

The Malcolm Baldrige National Quality Award (now the Baldrige Performance Excellence Program) has appealed to me from its 1987 beginning. I read about the award, attended conferences about it, and took the Baldrige Examiner training to learn all I could about this exciting approach.

I found the explanation of how the seven Baldrige categories work together using the bicycle model shown here to be especially intuitive. Created by Martin Stankard, an early Baldrige Examiner, the model shows that we, the bike riders, use Leadership, Strategy, and Customer focus to steer the bicycle. We use Workforce and Operations to pedal or power the bicycle, and we use Measurement, Analysis, and Knowledge as our road map. Finally, the Results are the speed, distance, and other measures of our bike ride. The Stankard bicycle model tells me that we cannot make progress if we don't make use of all the categories in a holistic way—that our accomplishments result from a unified approach. For anyone wanting to know more about the value of the Baldrige program, I recommend Kay Kendall's and Glenn Bodinson's excellent book, *Leading the Malcolm Baldrige Way: How World-Class Leaders Align Their Organizations to Deliver Exceptional Results*.

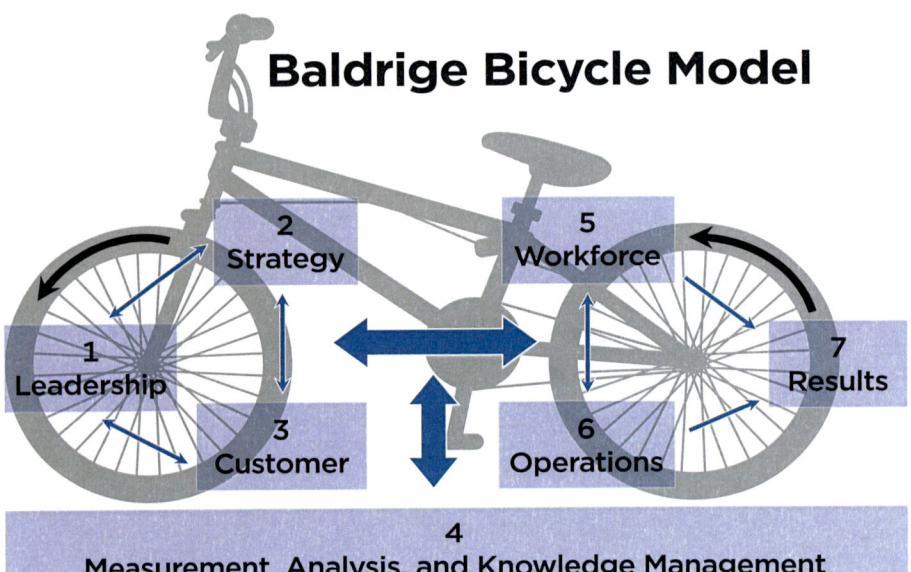

When I became CEO, I asked the senior members of Northeast Delta Dental's management team to take Baldrige-based Examiner training in the hope that they would become apostles. They did. Our Senior Vice President, Operations Bill Lambrukos said it was the best training he had ever had, and he became an ardent ambassador for Baldrige. Together, we invested in transforming our operations and processes using the Baldrige Category 6 operations principles.

Once we knew we could deliver, we were ready to introduce Northeast Delta Dental's Guarantee Of Service Excellence℠ (GOSE℠). Linda Roche, now Director of Account Services & Strategic Projects and former Director of Marketing, headed the internal GOSE℠ team. This focused everyone on customers and empowered everyone to do the right thing for their customers — both internal and external, as covered in the Customer Category 3. As a result of this continued focus on the customer, Northeast Delta Dental retains an amazing 98% of its customers annually, making us the top in the country, where the average group insurance retention rate is closer to 87%.

We didn't start with a customer retention rate of over 98%. We had to build to it with sustained attention and communication. I must admit that, for the first few years, using the Baldrige framework sometimes felt like marching into a strong headwind. To make GOSE^{SM} and other improvements work in our organization, I had to sell the ideas to two key stakeholder groups: our Board and our employees. To sell the idea to the Board, I showed them how well customers rated us and how we were growing the subscriber base.

To sell the ideas to our team of employees, our Vice President of Human Resources and I focused on increasing their job satisfaction, empowerment, and engagement as covered in the Workforce Category 5. We began by ensuring that pay and benefits were appropriate and equitable. Then we added job skills training on such topics as GOSE^{SM}, Baldrige, team building, values, and communication. With the intention of increasing employee empowerment, we provided training on management and leadership styles, created a respectful workplace with conflict management, and made management coaching from experts available to managers. Next, we encouraged more staff recognition by stressing in monthly management meetings the importance of acknowledging and thanking employees, of being mentors and coaches, and of celebrating successes. We communicated often and with transparency about operational and corporate results to create a shared culture and set of goals. Recently, we have added mindfulness training to reduce stress. The best part is that our employees feel proud of working here. They are not working just to get paid but also to serve their neighbors and communities.

As we made improvements for operations, customers, and workforce, we also worked on the Leadership and Strategy Categories 1 and 2 to guide our organization. We defined our vision, mission, and core values statement. While they have matured over time, they have always provided valuable guidance for everyone at Northeast Delta Dental.

Finally, we collected and communicated our Measurements (Category 4) and Results (Category 7). Of course, the measures have matured; but, as our results show, we have every reason to feel proud of our accomplishments and grateful for the guidance on best management practices from the Baldrige program.

The Payoff of Building the Foundation

This figure shows the amazing growth and results we obtained as we built the foundation for Northeast Delta Dental. As the number of covered lives more than tripled between 1995 and 2019, the revenues increased by almost 600%.

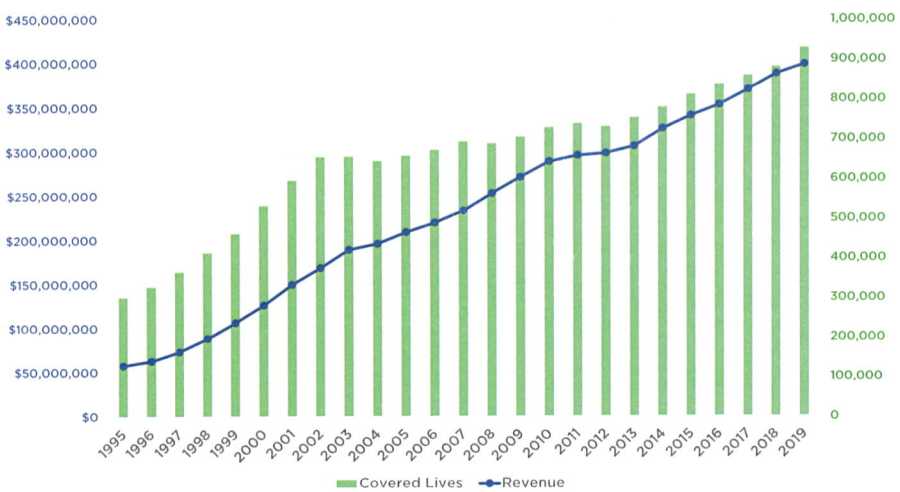

Building a Strong Foundation – Questions to Ask Yourself

1. Thinking about the ten elements of a strong foundation that I have described, how would you rate your organization on each one? On which ones is your organization strong, and on which ones does it need to improve?

2. For the elements that you think need improvement, would your colleagues agree with you? Would it make sense to discuss the elements with some trusted peers? Can you prioritize the elements that need improvement?

3. For which of the elements that need improvement do you have the most control or influence? Which improvements can you lead or make most easily?

4. How open is your organization to change? What would it take to persuade others to work with you on making needed improvements?

Section 2

During the Crisis

Use the Foundation to Act Wisely

About This Section

This section describes how we realized a crisis existed, how we decided on what actions to take to address the pandemic, and how we used different approaches for each of our stakeholder groups. I realize that the steps we took are unique to Northeast Delta Dental and would not make sense for all organizations. But I believe that certain of our decisions and actions — such as being guided by our mission and values, focusing on long-term goals rather than short-term profits, and communicating early and often with employees, customers, and other stakeholders — could apply to every organization.

Realize There Is a Crisis

It took a while for me to realize what the COVID-19 pandemic meant for Northeast Delta Dental. There were signs in January and February 2020 that there was a serious virus spreading around the world. To paraphrase Bill Gates and other visionaries, crises and trends are obvious in the rearview mirror but may be difficult to recognize when looking ahead.

So, when did I recognize that Northeast Delta Dental faced an existential crisis? On Sunday, March 8, 2020, I attended a Boston Celtics NBA game at the TD Garden along with over 19,000 other fans who were all screaming, sharing popcorn, and not wearing masks. It felt like life as usual, even though I had heard about the virus in the news.

It wasn't until Wednesday, March 11, that it really hit me. I was preparing to watch a basketball game on TV when the NBA announced that a player had COVID-19 and the game had to be canceled. Then they postponed the season. I think of the NBA as innovative and profit-oriented, so I was stunned by its decision. I thought, "If the NBA took that action, what is in store for Northeast Delta Dental?" I realized for the first time how serious this situation might become.

Our regular tri-state Northeast Delta Dental Board meeting was held as scheduled the next days on Thursday and Friday, March 12 and 13. It was held in person at our headquarters in Concord followed by a group dinner at a local hotel, with only four of the 42 Board members attending remotely. We followed our traditional March Board agenda, focusing on progress toward our strategic goals, our financials, and audit results. Our Pandemic Team held a general discussion about the virus on the evening of the twelfth, but only at the end of the Board meeting did the full Board devote about half an hour to talking hypothetically about what the "corona virus" (as we called it that day) might mean for us. Even though we didn't want to believe COVID-19 could be so serious, we wanted to be prudent. We talked mostly about the importance of wearing masks in our offices and about new processes that might be needed in dental offices. But really, it felt like business as usual, except for how empty the hotel was and for seeing people wearing masks.

It wasn't until Monday, March 16, just days after being with the over 19,000 other Celtics fans and participating in an almost normal Board meeting, that I realized we had a crisis and had to act. That was when the American Dental Association (ADA) issued recommendations that dental patients were only to be seen in emergencies. Regular medical visits — including most routine dental visits — were to be halted until further notice. That finally brought home the seriousness of the crisis for Northeast Delta Dental and our industry. (Fast forward to September 2021 — eighteen months later — the TD Garden announced that no one could enter the building without showing proof of vaccination. Who could have imagined?)

Looking back, I see that we had a period between March 11 and 16 when the world changed dramatically. Sure, there were inklings before that. But the trends were incremental. There was a wave forming, but we failed to catch the wave early. It was difficult to see what was happening until the wave became a tsunami. I see now that this is typical for industries that are about to undergo significant upheavals. They see the start of a trend but fail to realize how serious it will become and what it means for them. For example, taxi firms seemed to underestimate the impact of Uber and Lyft. Hotels underestimated the impact of Airbnb. And, I'm sorry to admit, Northeast Delta Dental was not the first to understand the impact of the virus.

On the other hand, we had a strategic plan and a disaster recovery plan for a pandemic, and so were much better prepared than many other organizations. I won't claim that we emerged a lot stronger after the pandemic, but I do know that we emerged in better shape than we would have if we had not laid a strong foundation and planned ahead.

I also learned that we had to be willing to plan and act amid great uncertainty: We had to accept ambiguity even though we would have greatly preferred certainty. None of us could forecast how the COVID virus would affect us, but we had to be comfortable making the best decisions we could based on the data — probably imperfect — that we had.

Prioritize Stakeholder Well-Being Over Profits

We were lucky that we already had a Pandemic Team in place and that they were quick to respond. We immediately closed the offices. Pandemic Team members were assigned specific responsibilities such as monitoring the news each day and getting out the word to senior leadership. Other members of the Team were responsible for determining what technology employees needed at home to work virtually and for understanding evolving employment guidelines. Of course, our number one priority was the safety of our employees.

Our Board procedures (regular Board meetings supplemented by interim meetings of the Executive Committees [ECs]) allowed us to act nimbly after we recognized the crisis. Sara Brehm, our Director of Board Relations & Executive Team, ensured we had available, and followed, proper Board management procedures during this time. The Pandemic Team and ECs met weekly for months and then shared their decisions for discussion and approval at the weekly management meetings and the quarterly full Board meetings. But these procedures would not have worked well if the Northeast Delta Dental executives and I had not already established trusting working relationships with the Board and EC members as described earlier.

At the first EC meeting, we talked about priorities. We considered our core values, which stress Communication, Teamwork, Quality, and Integrity. We also considered our main strategic goal, to grow the number of covered dental lives. In the pandemic, we saw no need to change this strategic goal but realized that it might take longer than originally planned to achieve.

And we considered how Northeast Delta Dental could help our participating dentists keep their offices open. We came up with a number of actions including providing masks and protective gear to the dentists and communicating to subscribers about the safety of returning for dental care. More on this later in this section.

In the end, we agreed our values, our strategic goals, and the actions we needed to take were complementary: We would put the well-being of all our stakeholders ahead of short-term profits (what we nonprofits call contribution to reserves).

That first week, we focused on employee safety. Our employees and communication with them had to come first. We felt nothing was more important than acting with integrity by doing the right thing. Putting the welfare of our employees ahead of any profit considerations (in accordance with our values), we immediately decided to send everyone (with a few essential exceptions) home, which involved physically clearing the offices and making sure even the most dedicated went home.

For the first ten days, some people took earned vacation time. After that, we gave everyone emergency sick leave to cover the cost of their lost time. Frank

Boucher, our Senior Vice President of Finance and CFO, came into the office every day after the shutdown and personally made sure the relief checks for our dentists and premium credits for our customers were sent out correctly. We also ensured that every employee had the necessary equipment, internet, and phone connections to stay in touch. When our dental claims work dropped as dental offices could only perform emergency work, and with no external events to manage, we did furlough several employees, almost all of whom returned when regular dentist visits resumed.

> *"We felt nothing was more important than acting with integrity by doing the right thing."*

During the next EC meeting on the week of March 23, when we knew our employees were safe, we focused on our dentists. How could we keep them financially sound when many patients stopped coming to their offices after the American Dental Association recommended on March 16 that dentists nationwide postpone elective procedures? One way to address this was to let dentists file claims with us for work that had begun but was not yet finished. For instance, dental crowns required multiple visits and are not historically paid by Northeast Delta Dental (or other insurers) until the conclusion of the final visit. We decided to pay upfront during the pandemic to help with their cash flow. We also considered how we could help keep dental personnel physically safe given the nature of the services they performed for the patients who did come in. That quickly led us to decide to purchase, and deliver in person, essential personal protection equipment (PPE), primarily masks and gowns. We also provided grants (not loans) to the dental community to help with cash flow in March and April. Ultimately, this was a $7 million investment in the dental community.

The dentists on our Boards were relentlessly generous with their time. Many (including former Board members) personally delivered PPE to our participating dentists.

Here's what Dr. Rabbath, Northeast Delta Dental Board member and President of the New Hampshire Academy of General Dentists had to say: "During the times when the pandemic forced dental offices to close and dental supplies were out of reach, the dental community was extremely thankful for the unprecedented relief headed by Tom Raffio and the Northeast Delta Dental Board. No one ever took such leadership in the rest of the United States."

By April and May, we were thinking about the welfare of our customers, meaning the people we insure. We knew that all our large employer customers who purchase Northeast Delta Dental's dental insurance for their employees were hurting as their revenues fell precipitously. We knew they could not afford their monthly premiums or administrative fees for long if they had greatly reduced incomes. Similarly, for individual subscribers, we knew that they could not afford their premiums if they were laid off. So, we decided to forgive some of their premiums. Under the leadership of our Vice President of Sales and Marketing and our Actuary, we worked to develop innovative ways to give relief to our customers. In the end, we decided that for all customers, whether individuals or large or small organizations, we would return or reduce their July 2020 premiums or September administrative fees. It sounds simple, but it took a huge bite out of our reserves because it cost almost $19 million.

After we decided not to collect the premiums, we realized this would affect our brokers, who are paid a percentage of the premiums they bring in. So, we resolved to pay their usual monthly commissions, notwithstanding. Of course, this affected our bottom line, but we felt it was the right thing to do to show the brokers how much we cared about their well-being and valued their service. This was a further $700,000 investment in our broker partners, usually small businesses themselves, to keep them strong during the pandemic.

Lastly, we turned our attention to what we could do for the general public in our communities. We knew every business was hurting, and nonprofits especially. We thought about the nonprofits and their staff members (often working for modest pay) and their clients who often had no dental coverage. As a result, Northeast Delta Dental decided on March 13 to give $500,000 in grants to help nonprofits in our states. The first $400,000 of that amount was made through our Foundation in grants related to oral health. We contacted the nonprofits to tell them they were approved and could use the funds in any way they needed to keep them safe and financially strong. This could be for equipment or administrative or overhead costs. The $100,000 balance of the grants came from the corporation and went to nonprofits unrelated to oral health, such as the arts and theater organizations we had supported in the past.

Ultimately, the Executive Committees and then the full Board authorized us to spend $27 million in the first six months to take care of our employees, dentists, customers and subscribers, brokers, and nonprofits whose staff and clients had no dental insurance. These expenditures were then approved by our regulators as needed.

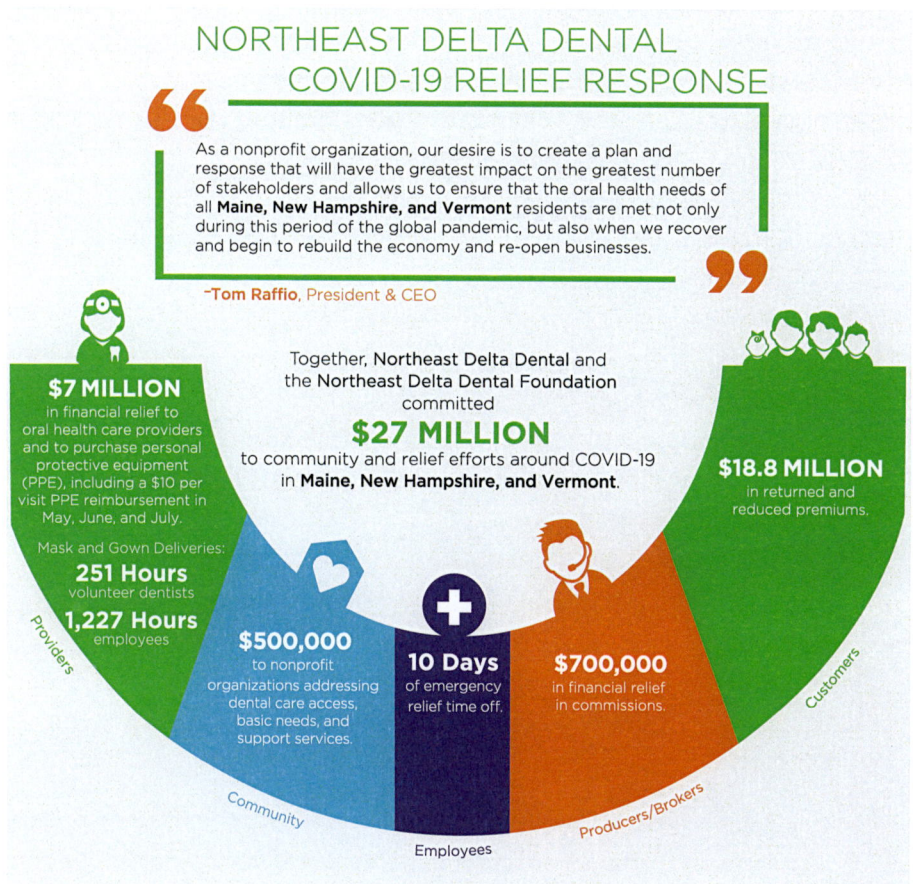

Thanks to Delta Dental of Colorado for this infographic format!

Get Board and Regulator Approval to Act

I realized that good governance required that any expenditures we were contemplating needed approval from our Boards, which wouldn't meet again for months.

As an insurance company, I knew we would be audited by the regulators and would need to prove we had the legal authority to act. Convening the full Boards with all 42 very busy members was impossible, but I was able to convene the 14 members of the Executive Committees rapidly. The Executive Committee meetings were always documented and sent to the full Boards for final approval. Our use of the Executive Committees allowed us to act quickly but prudently. I liked to say at the time and now, "Do it right. Be quick but don't rush," paraphrasing the famous words of legendary UCLA basketball coach, John Wooden.

In addition to the Executive Committee, a select group of Delta Dental Board members met frequently during the early part of the pandemic. They were called the Dream Team because they were so very helpful.

- Delta Dental Plan of New Hampshire (DDPNH) Executive Committee:
  - Dr. David Staples, DDPNH Board Chair
  - Dr. Richard Bolduc, DDPNH Board Vice Chair
  - Dr. Christiane Rothwangl
  - Mr. Matthew Cookson
  - Mr. James St. Jean, DDPNH Finance/Audit Committee Chair
- Delta Dental Plan of Maine (DDPME) and Delta Dental Plan of Vermont (DDPVT) Board Chairs:
  - Mr. Donald Oakes, former DDPME Board Chair
  - Dr. David Baasch, former DDPVT Board Chair
- Tri-State Professional Relations Committee (PRC) Chairs:
  - Dr. Jeffrey Doss, former DDPME PRC Chair
  - Dr. Jean-Paul Rabbath, former DDPNH PRC Chair
  - Dr. David Solomon, former DDPVT PRC Chair, and Board Vice Chair

About half the Executive Committee members had dental practices and saw their practice volumes plummet, so they were able and motivated to meet. Our first Executive Committee meeting was convened on Monday, March 16, by conference call. (We soon switched to Webex and Zoom like everyone else.) These frequent Executive Committee meetings continued through July 2020 when we resumed regularly scheduled Board meetings.

We were able to work with and convince our Board members and our regulators that we could afford these vast sums to help our stakeholders get through the crisis. Over the years, our long-term plan was always to build our reserves to protect us in the event of crises like this one. So, when this crisis hit, we were blessed with our substantial financial reserves and the trusting relationships we had developed with our Boards and regulators.

It turns out that giving away money is not easy for a not-for-profit insurance company. Two members of our leadership team were especially instrumental in getting approvals for the $27 million expenditure to support our stakeholders. Our Director of Board Relations & Executive Team, Sara Brehm, ensured we followed all the correct procedures with the Executive Committees and Boards when securing their approvals. The other was our General Counsel during the period, Erica Bodwell, who worked to secure all necessary legal approvals from our regulators. Once the pandemic slowed, Northeast Delta Dental underwent a huge routine Department of Insurance audit by the combined states of Maine, New Hampshire, and Vermont, which looked especially closely at whether we followed the necessary protocols in securing expenditure approvals. I am very grateful for the colleagues who made sure we followed them correctly.

In retrospect, our aid to all our stakeholders was impressive, but we could have given back even more and still have been fine. Our claims and other expenses dropped because people were not going to dentists except for emergencies. We were still very early in the first pandemic in over 100 years, so we felt we needed to be fiscally prudent and not go through our reserves too rapidly. While our actions showed that we did the right thing by prioritizing our stakeholders over profits, I still ask myself if we might have done more.

Communicate, Communicate, Communicate

Even as we were making massive operating and financial changes, we began immediately to focus on communicating with all our stakeholders. Videos, emails, electronic newsletters, website postings, and in some cases, direct mail were all used to keep external and internal stakeholders informed. For employees, I sent emails daily. For participating dentists, I communicated weekly. For the Board, I communicated daily for a while with the Executive Committee and almost as often with the other Board members. For the subscribers and community, I communicated when appropriate, at least monthly.

I think it's worthwhile to look in detail at how we served and communicated with each of our stakeholder groups. While we care deeply about them all, we used different methods for each. Please see the Appendix for examples of my communications to our employees, participating dentists, customers, and brokers.

Serve and Communicate with Employees

On March 16, we began sending employees home. We made sure everyone knew safety was our number one concern and that we were doing this with their well-being in mind. All employees immediately received 10 days of emergency time off to attend to their individual and family health needs.

All managers who supervised others participated in several online meetings with me that were mandatory in the early days of the crisis. For safety reasons, we developed a policy that employees were not to attend any external events that were sponsored by Northeast Delta Dental, that our financial contribution would be sufficient.

All meetings immediately became virtual, and we provided everyone with training in Webex for video conferencing. We were already using Webex rather than Zoom because it had great security measures. When Zoom increased its security, we began to use that service also, depending on participant preferences.

The first to work from home were the marketing and salespeople who already had PCs or iPads and phone connections at home and were used to working there when they weren't on the road or in the office.

When we saw claims dropping (as dentists had to close their offices), we were able to send most claims processing people home. By the end of March, in just two weeks, only about 35 essential people out of 232 employees were working in the office. Those who were in the office — including 15 in senior management and finance and 20 in customer service and mail room who were needed to implement our pandemic plans and handle incoming mail and calls — were widely spaced and masked. Because we operated in a space that normally accommodates hundreds, we were able to physically distance. Those who were not senior leaders were paid a roughly 15% premium for going the extra mile by working in the office.

The rest worked from home using whatever equipment they had. Then, when we could see that the crisis was a long-term phenomenon that would drag on for months, our Information Systems Support Team, led by Vice President Mike Bourbeau, began to personally deliver each person's office laptop or PC, often with printers and ergonomically designed seating, to them at home. Because of HIPAA privacy rules, all customer paperwork had to be printed out at home and then transported to the office to keep it secure. Within two months, everyone had what they needed to work effectively and comfortably at home.

Out of the 232 employees who were working on March 16, we only had to furlough 34. For the first month, we had everyone use extended sick pay. Frank Boucher, our Senior Vice President of Finance and CFO, came into the office each day to ensure that checks to suppliers, dentists, and brokers and premium credits to group customers and subscribers were calculated correctly and distributed promptly. And Bonnie St. Lawrence, a Human Resources teammate, managed the details of our employees' payroll and benefits very adeptly even while working from home.

When we saw that the extended sick pay could not outlast the pandemic, we reluctantly had to extend the furlough for some. I communicated daily with the furloughed and non-furloughed employees (sometimes multiple times a day) by email and phone. I talked a lot about their safety and health and about the drops in the numbers of claims and calls that are our livelihood. This ensured they understood our financial situation and the necessity of furloughs.

Our Vice President of Human Resources, Connie Roy-Czyzowski, called those furloughed almost daily and helped them apply for unemployment insurance. Though working from home, she often spent up to 16 hours a day contacting employees.

The good news, which we shared with all employees, was that dentists were allowed to reopen in all three states between mid and late May. We were lucky — much luckier than many industries. This meant that we could see a way to put almost everyone back to work by June.

In the end, we lost only five employees. Three retired, and two whose roles required in-person meetings outside the office were reluctantly told we could not see the need for events for a year or so. The effect of our intense and honest communications with these employees was that we had no resignations and were even thanked by those we had to furlough for our care and support.

To further support our employees through this challenging time, we provided ongoing training classes for professional development. We also created special sections in our employee newsletter where employees could share personal tips for working during the pandemic and suggestions for books, interesting podcasts, or favorite movies and TV shows.

We also gave premium pay to those employees who needed to come to the office in person during the height of the pandemic. For all employees, we continued to add to their retirement funds and added extra cash bonuses because of their criticality at the start of the pandemic.

To communicate with our employees, I used a combination of emails, conference calls, and Zoom, reaching out daily about important matters. Also, since the start of COVID, I have written notes on and mailed birthday cards to every employee, which they tell me has been a huge boost to them as they work virtually. See the Appendix for examples of my internal communications during the crisis.

- Everyone at every level was encouraged to care for themselves, their families, their pets, and their neighbors. For example, employees were told they could miss three hours of work to set their children up on Zoom for school or to drive across town to make sure their parents had food or masks. A consistent message was the importance of taking care of oneself and others.
- We created a Parent Support Group that met biweekly on company time from mid-January through mid-June 2021. Working parents could discuss ways to handle parenting challenges and how best to take care of themselves and their children. Participants told us they found the group very valuable and that it helped them get through this time of great stress.
- Our monthly *Team Power* newsletter kept us all informed and on the same wavelength. It included the latest news from the CFO and other managers, as well as tips and news of each other.
- We listened to and learned from our stakeholders how we could best help them through this public health crisis. One way was to expand our communication channels to include a COVID-19 microsite. This dedicated area on our website provided regular updates, helpful tips for continuing services through the pandemic, and contact information for our stakeholders to reach out directly to our team and me if they had questions or concerns.

DURING THE CRISIS

One of the best aspects of our steady drumbeat of communications with employees was that it helped reduce the feelings of isolation that so many people experienced during the pandemic. My goal in the daily communications with them was to create a sense of family so that everyone felt included and valued and knew that we wanted them to take care of themselves first so they could take care of others. By the end of 2020, I had sent over 200 emails to our employees and was delighted to hear from one who reported, *"I have kept every one of your 200 emails in an email folder. Have a wonderful day!"*

Another benefit of my daily communications with employees was that it kept them in the loop on the future well-being of Northeast Delta Dental. This was important because they all naturally worried about how the pandemic would affect their job security. We were able to reassure them that Northeast Delta Dental was on top of the situation and was doing fine. It gave them confidence in their futures with Northeast Delta Dental and limited their turnover when many organizations were struggling to keep valued employees. A white paper by the Prevedere consulting firm, *The New Link between Personal Job Security and Corporate Business Plans*, supports my belief in the connection between employee retention and communication about the organization's plans.

After the first week or two, we settled in for the long haul. I continued my daily emails and personally visited everyone I could in the office. Some examples of my emails are included in the Appendix. They show that, in keeping with my servant leader style, I emphasized keeping them healthy and fit and personalized the message with photos of my granddaughter, who was only 14 months in March 2020 and has grown in front of the staff during the pandemic. She is so popular that when I don't send pictures, people let me know they miss them.

These photos bookended my communications in 2020 and 2021. They showed how I conveyed my sense that we were all family by including my granddaughter, Havanna. How we all changed during that year!

2020

2021

Here are some responses about Havanna from two employees:

> I really appreciate all the serious and important content in all of your emails, but I have to say the best part is the various activities of your granddaughter. I'm happy that you have this time with your granddaughter and seeing the pictures always gives me a smile or a giggle. Thanks.

• • •

> I hope all is well with you and your lovely family. I'm enjoying all the pictures that you send in your daily COVID-19 emails. Please keep them coming!

As time passed, my messages became more and more upbeat. I was gratified to hear from many employees how my confidence in the future of Northeast Delta Dental and my genuine caring had sustained them. Here are letters I received talking about how well our new digital work processes were going:

> I like working from home, but I am missing working at the office, miss seeing my colleagues in person. Good thing we have Zoom or Webex meetings as it gives a great opportunity to interact with these uneasy times going on.

• • •

> Good Morning Tom,
>
> First, thank you for the generous birthday/anniversary gift and the accompanying card. This is very thoughtful and much appreciated. I am always amazed how you take the time to sign each card yourself.
>
> I truly like working from home. I find myself to be more productive, do not need to take a day off due to weather, and more apt to volunteer to work on weekends if the need arises, since I don't have to leave my home.
>
> The biggest improvement in our department is sending all documents by email. Documents that would normally be mailed to groups, (contract applications, group contracts, addendum letters, etc.) are now being emailed in PDF format. When we first started emailing documents both groups and producers had commented how much better and efficient this is. I have noticed that by sending documents electronically we are also receiving them back signed quickly,

sometimes within an hour of sending them. Going electronic is a great way of reducing waste and cost of paper and mailing.

Thank you for taking the time to listen and hear your employees.

This is another letter about how much people appreciated being able to work from home:

Hi Tom,

I remember a year ago when this all happened, and thinking how is all of us working from home going to work? How nervous that something like this could actually happen to the whole country, the whole world. It was really the weirdest thing I could have imagined. Then you, and Senior Management acting so quickly to keep us all safe and help reassure us that we'd find a way to make this all work, making sure everyone had whatever technology we needed and desks, chairs, etc. The Zoom meetings so we could all stay connected and your daily email updates, have made a world of difference. We are so lucky to (most of us) not have had any disruption to our employment. It was pretty remarkable that the disruption was so minimal.

Working from home has been an interesting experience, not as bad as I had thought it would be. I'll admit on those snow days, it was nice to know I didn't have to drive 45 min to work. We're able to retain our business and sell new business, have meetings, etc. Personally, I feel bad for my youngest son, Ian, having to finish his Senior year at college on-line at home and they will not be having a commencement; but as I try to point out to him, his class has proven that they are resilient and flexible, great qualities for the workforce.

I cannot wait until we can all get together again (what an epic Employee Appreciation Event the next one we can have will be) without having to wear masks all the time and be able to hug our friends and co-workers. Thank you for being the rock to hold us together and sharing your granddaughter with us to put a smile on our face every morning. I feel lucky indeed. Thanks again.

And here are two of my favorite letters. They make me feel that all my communications have been worthwhile:

> Tom, I was talking to a group last night about being ... and staying ... positive, and I commented that you are the leader in this category. This past year for me has been of highs and lows, from being furloughed last April to being able to return in June, to being ... concerned I was going to contract this dreaded virus, and worried that I would have to use earned time if I had to quarantine, to recently having the ability ... to work from home.
>
> The one steady point of this past year has been YOU. When this pandemic hit, no one knew what to expect and how long it was going to last, but it was your reassuring words in your detail emails to us that the companies were going to be fine and get through this ... Your leadership has been that of being cool under pressure, being reassuring that we were going to survive and be better for it.
>
> I want to thank you personally for giving me the confidence to move forward every day when some days it seemed like I couldn't do it. I have never worked for a company that looked out for their employees more than Northeast Delta Dental does, and you should be extremely proud of this!

· · ·

> Hi Tom,
>
> As we've chatted about previously — It really stands out how above and beyond Northeast Delta Dental went to support everyone from the providers losing business to the customers scared of losing their coverage. I love New Hampshire, so it's meaningful to see how Northeast Delta Dental has its (plus Maine's and Vermont's) back.
>
> I've never worked somewhere so holistic in their approach to serving the whole community, and every time we get a recognition like this, it's an additional validation of all that we do.
>
> Even in such a year as difficult as 2020, to get an additional 2% on top of the 3% blew my mind and made me tear up a bit. We really, as a team here, took all the lemons given to us and made lemonade ... So, thanks for all you and everyone else here at Northeast Delta Dental does, Tom. It's a blessing to be a part of what we do, recognitions or not.

I believe that our honest and consistent communication with our employees, as well as our caring policies, have been responsible for us maintaining our excellent results in the annual employee engagement survey. This survey is conducted by *Business NH Magazine* among the firms applying to be judged best place to work in New Hampshire. We already showed earlier how well we were doing before the pandemic, and this chart's results for 2021 show that we maintained and even improved our scores during the pandemic. I like to say Northeast Delta Dental remains the cream of the crop in employee engagement.

Survey Metric	Northeast Delta Dental Avg. Score 2016-20	Northeast Delta Dental Score 2021	Amt. Northeast Delta Dental Scores Above Norm in 2021
Highly engaged	80%	81%	17%
It starts at the top	86%	91%	17%
Overall (across all metrics)	86%	87%	11%
Communication	89%	90%	14%

Communicate with the Board and Regulators

In March 2020, when the crisis began, I communicated almost daily with our Executive Committees and the full Board. I talked about what we were doing to keep every one of our stakeholder groups safe physically and financially. I talked about our goals in terms of our mission, values, and strategy and how we were living them even during the crisis. When the ECs met, I shared their thinking with the other Board members. All this communication (mostly via emails, Webex, and Zoom) meant that when I asked for EC and Board support for the actions we planned, there was a consensus about what to do. The tone was not as family oriented as for the employees, but it was warmly professional.

Over time, as the pandemic wore on, my communications to the Board tapered, switching from daily, to weekly, to monthly. I talked less about safety and more about how we were going to resume working toward our strategic goals, like growth and diversity. By July 2020, we resumed our regular Board meeting schedule (although by Zoom). One of our strategic priorities for 2020 was Diversity, Equity, and Inclusion and addressing the disparities in dental care across ethnic groups. We continued to work on this oral health care disparity project throughout the pandemic, which put us in a good position to continue to make progress on this sensitive issue. Most recently, the Boards agreed to invest $6 million in a dentist student loan repayment program and another $350,000 to address shortages of hygienists and dental assistants.

For the regulators, we needed their approval to implement a number of our plans, so we used a combination of phone calls and Zoom meetings to make our case for giving premium relief to our subscribers and group employers. It was an easy sell for two reasons. One, we had built up a trusting relationship with the regulators over time, so they were willing to act quickly and positively. Two, forgiving the July 2020 premiums was a positive action that reflected well on Northeast Delta Dental and the regulators who gave approval. Similarly, we informed regulators of our plan to continue to pay the broker commissions for July even though we were not collecting the premiums that month.

Although we did not need regulator approval for the financial and PPE aid we gave to our participating dentists and the donations our Foundation made to nonprofits, we kept the regulators informed. This was important because we were dipping into our cash reserves. We showed that we could afford to give the aid to help keep our dentists and others afloat.

Serve and Communicate with Participating Dentists

For participating dentists, I communicated weekly throughout the entire COVID-19 crisis. Dentist offices in all three of our states closed on March 16, 2020, except for emergency dental care. They, like everyone else, had to understand how to keep themselves and their patients safe before they could reopen.

The dental office reopenings occurred about two months later in May 2020, following each state's governor's safety protocols: May 11 in New Hampshire, May 18 in Maine, and May 26 through June 1 in Vermont. Masking was a key requirement. PPE and other infection control protocols were crucial. Recall, Northeast Delta Dental had helped by providing free or discounted PPE to dentists to aid in their pursuit of reopening safely.

As I mentioned earlier, to be prepared for a pandemic, we had purchased hundreds of blue surgical masks for our staff long before COVID-19 hit. You'd think we were in great shape. But, when the pandemic hit in March, Dr. Fauci emphasized distancing and hand sanitation but not necessarily masking. We operate near the major teaching hospital serving New Hampshire and Vermont (Dartmouth-Hitchcock Medical Center); and, when that hospital put out pleas for masks, we felt that their need was much greater than ours.

Since we only had about 35 people coming into the office (20 in customer service and mail room and 15 in management and finance), we felt we could get by without all the masks and drove them ourselves over to Dartmouth-Hitchcock. We felt very good about our contribution until we gradually learned the importance of masking and that our staff and our dentists were also in need. In hindsight, we probably should have kept many of the masks for our own people to use, but we felt compelled to assist our frontline medical personnel first.

My takeaway from this adventure of mask allocation is that even when excellent disaster planning is done, at the beginning of each disaster we may lack perfect information and may make some decisions we later question. We must do the best we can with the information available at the time, while following best practice protocols.

Because we had already purchased surgical masks and established a relationship with our vendor, SoClean®, who was already one of our group dental insurance customers, we were able to order and receive 110,000 additional KN95 masks. We put these in one of our vacated headquarters buildings to be distributed to our dentists by the time they were ready to reopen. This sounds much easier than it was. Many dentists had closed their offices and were working remotely on an emergency basis. So, we couldn't just ship the masks. We had to learn where to deliver the masks and then determine how to send them safely and securely. How?

The heroes were our Board members, especially the Board members who are dentists, and our in-office staff members. This included former Board Chairs Dr. Paul Averill (DDPVT) and Dr. Jeffrey Doss (DDPME). They contacted the dentists to get drop-off addresses (often at their homes) and then drove the masks to them. The dentist Board members alone donated 251 hours of their time to deliver the PPE! Two of our state Board Chairs — Dr. David Solomon of Vermont and Dr. David Staples of New Hampshire — hand delivered masks and gowns to dozens of participating dentists' offices and homes. They shared that not only did they enjoy the opportunity to meet many of the dentists and staff members, they were often a valuable source of information for the offices not yet up to speed on all the various mandates from state and federal agencies. I think this demonstrates how the foundation laid in nurturing and engaging a well-informed and hardworking board can pay off during a crisis.

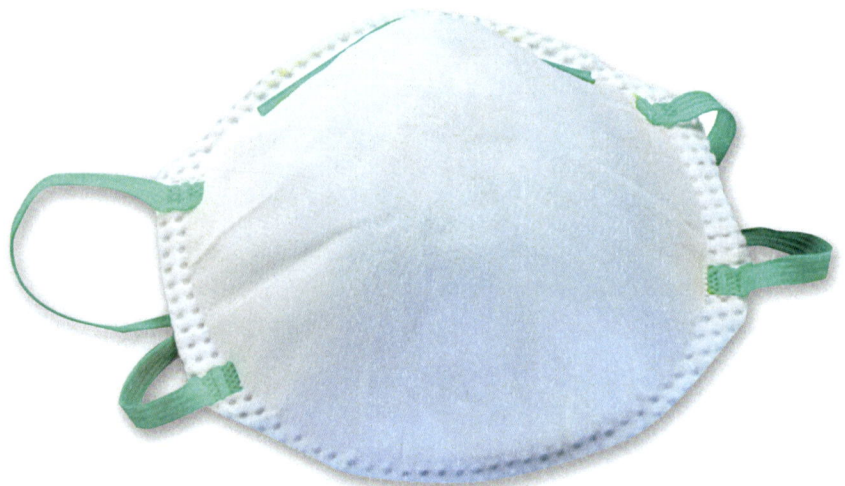

In 2020 and the first half of 2021, we packaged and shipped thousands of PPE to our participating dentists.
- 113,000+ KN95 and N95 masks
- 9,000+ reusable gowns
- 3,200+ boxes of nitrile gloves

I received many, many grateful letters and notes, often handwritten, from our participating dentists and their office staff. Here are some of my favorites:

> *Thank you again and your great company for your continued support in sending the N95 masks. They are so needed, and we are grateful to you. This will allow us to continue to care for the citizens of New Hampshire.*

• • •

> *What a welcome surprise when I came to my office and found the box of KN95 masks which you donated. I have always said Northeast Delta Dental is the best insurance company that we deal with, and this certainly proved it.*

We were also able to help financially. Northeast Delta Dental approved a relief package for all currently participating network dentists and oral surgeons, equating to approximately one percent of the 2019 claim payments for each office. This totaled $4.3 million in direct financial relief. We also adjusted claims from our PPO providers between mid-February and March 17, 2020, to Premier rates, with the amount of the difference between PPO and Premier rates calculated and paid as a second form of relief.

We received many notes of thanks for our financial assistance:

> *I wanted to write to you to share my sincere gratitude from myself, my family, and all the dentists of New Hampshire for you "stepping up to the plate" by your well needed financial assistance. Thank you also for having this sent so quickly. Every little bit helps. I would like to wish you good health and safety to you and your family during these difficult and unusual times.*
>
> • • •
>
> *Thank you to you and Delta Dental for the relief payment I received. It was a very nice gesture on your part. During these difficult times it is important that people remain calm and act with kindness, which you have done. I am doing my best also ... by treating emergency patients at my office for a discounted fee ... It's all about kindness. Keep up the good work.*
>
> • • •
>
> *I wanted to extend a personal thank you for the disaster relief payment that was recently sent to my office. Acts like this exemplify the underlying good intentions of Northeast Delta Dental. Thank you for reminding me that we are all in this together. It is my belief that we shall emerge from this pandemic stronger and more united. Best wishes from my team to yours.*

This letter about how one young Maine dentist sees our relationship is especially rewarding:

> *I am sending you a thank you email for continually blessing our path with your outreach and support in our quest to become better and more successful at what we do. You truly have set a benchmark for what this relationship could be like, and I absolutely appreciate your vision and approach. It is always wonderful to hear from you.*

This graph shows the precipitous drop in dental claims in New Hampshire (echoed in Maine and Vermont) in 2020 (the blue line) and how it is coming back strong in 2021. This means that our participating dentists and their patients have weathered the pandemic and are back on track to achieving healthy smiles.

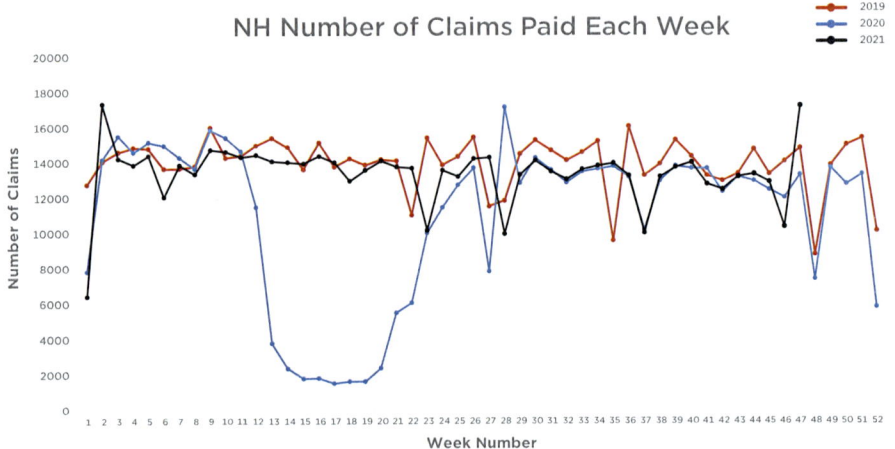

Serve and Communicate with Customers

The COVID-19 pandemic naturally brought uncertainty to our many valued group clients and individual subscribers. The customers' questions included: What if I need to see a dentist during this time? Will my claims still be paid? What will happen if I get furloughed from my job?

To answer these questions, Northeast Delta Dental instituted several initiatives to help relieve employers, their people, and our individual customers from worry. Starting with our website, we created TED Talk-like videos explaining what was happening and answering frequently asked COVID-19 questions. My role model was FDR's fireside chats, where he explained the situation in simple, straightforward terms. We acknowledged that they might be worried about getting needed dental care and reassured them that their dentists could still operate on an emergency basis. We provided a phone number to call us if they needed help getting an appointment. We also provided links to important information, such as tips for maintaining good oral health at home during the pandemic.

Importantly, we reassured our members that if they needed to see a dentist — even when most visits were limited to emergencies — that their claims would be processed. While most of our employees worked from home, we remained open for business. Despite a visit to the dentist looking and feeling different due to the precautions needed to keep patients safe, our systems for processing group and individual claims and paying dentists remained largely unchanged.

When we had approval from our Executive Committees, our full Board, and regulators, we were ready to announce our premium forgiveness program. We did this with direct communications to all group and individual customers in a letter from me telling them exactly how much of their July 2020 premium would be forgiven. In most cases, it was 100%. Please see the Appendix for a sample of my letter to subscribers and some reactions from grateful customers.

Then, as we neared the start of 2021, we made another generous decision to help group and individual subscribers who might be hurting financially. We instituted a "rate hold," meaning we did not add our usual 3-7% rate increase to their premiums. We held their rates steady, with no increase, even though we were experiencing a rise in dental claims as patients with pent-up issues flocked to their dentists. We expect to see losses in our Northeast Delta Dental revenue stream for 2021, although we won't know exactly how much until the end of 2021. Whatever we lose, we know we will feel good about helping our customers.

Here is a handwritten letter of thanks in July from an individual subscriber:

Dear Delta Dental,

Who does this?! Thank you so very much for the waiver of a payment on our plan! It is so thoughtful! At such a needed time. I would love to yell this to the world! Thank you.

And this is a June letter from the president of one of our larger corporate customers. I especially appreciate that he says Northeast Delta Dental will be his "dentistry partner" in the future.

Dear Mr. Raffio,

I truly hope you and your family, and the entire Delta Dental team have remained safe and healthy.

I just wanted to sincerely thank you for the free month of Dental coverage in July. It has been a very challenging time for all of us. We are so grateful for your generosity and cannot thank you enough.

Northeast Delta Dental will surely be our dentistry partner for a long time to come.

Have a great rest of 2020 and again thanks so much for this gift and additionally for the great service your organization provides. I have always told my employees — "Northeast Delta Dental is the Cadillac of dental insurance providers," and I really mean it.

During 2020, tri-state Northeast Delta Dental held three of the top five customer retention rates in the entire Delta Dental System. Vermont was ranked first, Maine second, and New Hampshire fifth. Those rankings are positions we've maintained since 2018, but our retention rate actually increased in 2020. We think this reflects the loyalty we earned through our relief efforts and our industry-leading Health through Oral Wellness® (HOW®) program.

However, I must admit that we do sometimes lose customers to lower-cost commercial carriers. Usually, we welcome back these lost customers within a year or two because they miss our excellent service, broad network of participating dentists, and our HOW® program. For example, in Vermont, both the Community Health Centers of Burlington and Northern Counties Health Care recently returned to Northeast Delta Dental after experiencing dental coverage with one of our for-profit commercial competitors.

Serve and Communicate with Brokers and Benefit Consultants

From the time the crisis hit in mid-March, we felt we were in partnership with the brokers and benefit consultants because we both cared about the well-being of our common customers, the group and individual customers who purchased insurance from us. The Northeast Delta Dental marketing team and I stayed in frequent contact and dialog with the brokers, mainly using a combination of phone conversations, personal emails, and some group emails. Once we decided to relieve the customers by forgiving their July 2020 premiums, we decided it was only right to pay our brokers their commissions. In all, we paid them $700,000 extra in commissions and financial relief. Please see the Appendix for a group email.

Needless to say, the brokers were thankful. The following notes are typical of those we received:

Good Afternoon Tom,

On behalf of (Company Name) and our very happy, mutual Northeast Delta Dental clients, I wanted to say how much I appreciate all that Northeast Delta Dental has done for everyone in our community. I read your well-crafted message and it reminds me what a great community partner Northeast Delta Dental is.

I did have one of my groups, just today, acknowledge the $0.00 due for July and they were appreciative.

We continue to partner in our community and within our working families and relating families to get through this together. With the first day of summer fast approaching and the midpoint of the 2020 year, we can all only hope things are going to be better, maybe different, but improved as compared to the first six months of this year.

Thanks again for the collaborative partnership.

· · ·

Tom, Well done, excellent work. Proud to be a partner of your firm!

· · ·

Thank you very much, Tom. As much as you appreciate us, we appreciate you more!

Serve and Communicate with Communities

A big part of our community-focused response was using any and all ways to keep our subscribers and the community informed and encouraged during the pandemic. We provided regular email and *Oral Health Newsletter* updates to over 135,000 subscribers. Beginning in early July, I wrote a number of op-eds, letters to the editor, and blogs (see the Appendix) and did radio shows so people knew when it was safe to go to the dentist and what to expect before, during, and after their visits. I had to repeat the safety messages in August and afterward because some community members were confused by competing opinions. Our website and its videos remained vital sources of information and updates throughout the pandemic.

One of our most important programs has been the SMILES campaign featuring a video and a series of supporting print ads. This campaign sends an important and meaningful message to our communities: that from six feet away, we can still smile at each other and remind ourselves that we are still here for one another.

A grant from the Northeast Delta Dental Foundation helped Vermont Head Start to support a statewide "Tooth Tutors" program, promoting positive oral health practices for more than 900 Head Start/Early Head Start children and their families. This program connects children to dental providers in their communities to improve access to preventive oral health care. It also works with the dental community to better meet the needs of program participants.

In Maine, we donated more than 50,000 dental kits to the Partnership for Children's Oral Health, whose mission is to ensure that all Maine children can grow up free from preventable dental disease. Each kit contained a toothbrush, toothpaste, and floss in a bag. In total, the kits were distributed to 124 schools/school districts and 21 food cupboards.

In addition to all our pandemic-related initiatives, Northeast Delta Dental continued to provide the community support and education vital to promoting good oral health and overall wellness across all three of our states. We continued to give grants for dental equipment and receive letters of thanks from recipients:

> Thank you very much for the grant award. We will plan to go ahead and purchase the electric drill system and dental surgery instruments in the next 60 days... While the clinic closing is unfortunate, we are able to see people with dental emergencies and I think that it's a perfect time to take delivery on the new oral surgery equipment.

• • •

> We very much want to continue with our program, offering initial exams, x-rays and treatment planning, and cleanings, for low income and seniors without access to insurance coverage/funding... We will proceed now with outreach to the eligible population and begin getting them scheduled for as soon as the offices open again (which we hope will be sooner rather than later).

We maintained a strong presence on social media and through our online channels, the *Oral Health Update* and *Smile Coach Monthly*, and our popular print publications — the quarterly *Grin! Magazine* and *Grin! for Kids* activity book.

The Northeast Delta Dental Foundation paid out over $400,000 in grants to oral health-related nonprofts in 2020. And, Northeast Delta Dental corporation donated over $100,000 that year to nonprofits related to oral health, the arts, or other causes to help them get through the pandemic. While every recipient wrote thank you letters that were always heartfelt and pointed to the excellent work that our funding helped them accomplish, some letters stand out for me. This one was handwritten:

Dear Mr. Raffio,

I appreciate you taking the time to write me a congratulatory letter! My work means a lot to me, and being recognized by the Chamber and my peers has recommitted me to continue helping others. Thank you for your many years of support to Granite United Way and the Dismas Home of New Hampshire! I feel so fortunate to get to work in a community with you in it.

Some letters, like this one, move me because they show our recipients recognize our shared goal is to bring people together as a community:

Dear Tom,

Through your kindness and generosity, you exemplify an important lesson we have learned over the past year. **Together, we make a stronger, more inclusive community***... Tom, you have shown us what it means to come together as a community. Thanks to you, we are able to sustain our work and provide vital services to the veterans, service members, and their families during these challenging times.*

Please see the Appendix for examples of our communications with the public and nonprofits.

Questions About Your Response to COVID

1. What actions has your organization taken during the COVID pandemic that have been especially helpful? Why have they worked? How do you know?

2. Of the actions that Northeast Dental took, which have your organization not used? Which of these missing actions might be most helpful to your organization to undertake now?

3. Are there any actions your organization has taken that have been counterproductive? Is there any way to undo them?

4. What are the goals and values that have guided your organization during COVID so far? If they are not in writing, perhaps they are unwritten but well understood. And, how effective have they been in keeping your organization strong during the pandemic?

Section 3

Emerging from the Crisis

Renew the Foundation with Lessons Learned

At the Root Canal Connecting Our Two Headquarters Buildings with Actuary, Courtney Morin, FSA, the Financial Architect of our Stakeholder Relief (Left) and Connie Roy-Czyzowski, VP, Human Resources (Right)

About This Section

The first part of this section describes the actions we are taking in 2021 to continue to perform up to our high standards, even as we are uncertain if and when this crisis will pass. The second part describes my conclusions about how organizations can successfully emerge strong and resilient from a crisis like COVID. Finally, since this pandemic is not over and other disasters can occur, the section concludes by considering how to build a stronger foundation for your organization even during a crisis.

The Initial Recovery Process

The core of what we do as a not-for-profit insurer is paying dental claims, so we track the number of claims we pay each month by state very closely. An earlier graph showed how the number of claims dropped precipitously in the spring of 2020 when the pandemic hit. When that happened, our entire focus was on being innovative in maintaining our service and offering relief to all our stakeholders.

But then the number of claims filed gradually resumed. It reached the point, beginning in August of 2020 through the winter of 2021, when we saw that the number of claims filed was growing back to pre-pandemic levels. As we saw the volume of business resume, we began asking ourselves what to do next? What should we do about bringing back our employees? What would they want?

An analysis of the feedback from all our employees in the spring and summer of 2020 showed that almost everyone expressed that they missed seeing others in person and wanted to return to the office as quickly and safely as possible. In fact, when we realized that the isolation had become a mental health issue for some employees, we engaged famous speakers on coping with stress and depression, such as former New Hampshire Supreme Court Justice John T. Broderick and Dennis Gillan, a well-known speaker on mental health and suicide prevention. Their talks at our All Employees Meetings really helped employees cope. Gradually, this isolation depression quieted, and we heard more and more people saying that they liked working from home and wanted to continue.

So, in May 2021, to determine what our return philosophy should be, our Human Resources Vice President surveyed all our managers, directors, VPs, and the COO and CEO (me) about what we thought our direct reports would want to do. Which colleagues would prefer to work virtually, and which would prefer to return to the office? And, if they would prefer to return in person, where in the office layout would it make sense to have them seated? Based on their feedback, we made a tentative recovery plan that distinguished among different work groups.

- **Operations (claims processing):** Most of these employees prefer to continue working from home. They are more efficient this way and produce less paper. It is relatively easy to manage their work because we can see how efficiently and accurately they process their claims. Overall, the Operations group is planning a hybrid model where they work mostly from home but a portion of them come into the office every two weeks for a team meeting. We don't have everyone come to each team meeting in order to save space and limit the possible spread of illnesses. On the other hand, having everyone come in periodically means that people can maintain their personal connections and, we hope, maintain our strong culture.

- **Customer Service:** All of these people worked in the office before the pandemic. Around 20 came to the office during the pandemic and received premium pay because of the risk to their health and the unknowns. We verified that the customer service representatives who worked from home had the technology they needed (including our new automatic call distribution system and sufficient internet connections). When they were up to speed technically, we found that they performed even better than when in the office in person. For instance, in June 2021, they achieved an answer speed of just 18 seconds and an abandoned call rate of only 1.5% (which is considered nearly perfect since some calls are wrong numbers). Many of the customer service representatives have told us their health has never been better since they have been able to exercise more and commute less. So, it is not surprising that most of them prefer to continue working remotely.
- **Marketing and Sales:** When the pandemic made personal sales and marketing visits impossible, marketers tried new, often digital, ways to connect and engage with prospects and customers. Visits to restaurants and customer offices had to stop, but marketers found ways to interact personally with their contacts. Since we found that it was still possible to have the human touch remotely, the marketing team has opted to continue functioning from home.
- **Professional Relations:** This group handles the relationship with all the participating dentists in our network. Before the pandemic, they did this by calling on the dentists in person. Now, like the marketing and sales group, they have found new ways of engaging with their dentists digitally. They are delighted to remain working remotely because, during the pandemic, they added several dentists and retained our robust network. And, as CEO, I'm happy to see that the professional relations and the marketing/sales groups have become both more efficient and more effective as they have embraced digital engagement methods.

- **Information Systems:** The IS group functioned remotely before the pandemic, continued that way, and will remain remote in the future.
- **Legal and Compliance:** This group came in person to the office before the pandemic but operated very effectively from home during the pandemic. They have opted to remain remote in the future.
- **Support Services:** This group includes primarily the mailroom employees who needed to come into the office in person to deal with the paperwork. They understood that this was essential, although the volume of paper has decreased over time as the use of technology has increased. They will continue to be needed in person at the office.
- **Managers/Directors/VPs:** Most of our managers and directors could supervise their colleagues virtually and were happy to work from home. Most say they still are. But we are concerned whether working from home will allow younger people to move up the management ladder. Will they be able to make the contacts they want, be visible, learn from those more senior, drop in on me and others to make themselves known, and see what good leadership looks like? We are going to watch this carefully.

As I write this, the world is realizing that the pandemic is not over, as cases have surged. Our Pandemic Committee has just recommended delaying return to work on campus because of rising COVID Delta variant incidents. Fortunately, our return to work policy means that employees don't have to come back to campus in person unless they want to. We hear that some employees are eager to return, primarily because they miss connecting with their colleagues. On the other hand, we also know that other employees are reluctant to return because they are afraid of contracting COVID-19 themselves or bringing it home to their families. In the end, I'm glad we are able to leave the choice to most employees.

As our Human Resources Vice President put it, "The return to work is a process, not an event. As we gather information ... we may refine and amend the processes, policies, and tools necessary to make for a successful transition." In other words, this is still a work in progress. And, we continue to have many open issues that require close monitoring. For instance:

- If employees want to work a hybrid schedule (some full days in the office and some remote), should we issue them laptops to be carried between locations or provide PCs at both locations? This should be relatively easy to solve.

- How can we maintain and grow our use of technology? Professor Scott Galloway, author of the excellent book, *Post Corona: From Crisis to Opportunity*, and many other experts have observed that working remotely has spurred the need for new technologies, and this has spurred improved daily work procedures. The pandemic accelerated the use of technology (which was already happening gradually) to reduce non-value-added work. For instance, with fewer people available to answer our phones, we saw the customers and dentists making increased use of our website. As we improved the website and stakeholders learned how easy it was to use and that it was available 24/7, the website traffic grew, and call quality and speed of answer reached record levels. We need to remain attentive so that the technological muscle strength we have built during the pandemic remains powerful and continues to grow, augmenting our personal touch — not replacing it.
- How can we maintain personal connections with so many working remotely? When the campus reopens, we expect to have no more than 40% of our approximately 200 employees in the office on any given day. During the pandemic, we continued to hold our All Employees Meeting monthly. Instead of having them in person, we held them by Zoom. Our plan now is to continue that schedule but to have 150 employees participate remotely while 50 (who rotate) come in person to the meeting. By rotating who attends in person, eventually everyone should encounter their colleagues every few months, which we hope will be sufficient to maintain the personal connections that we have worked hard to build.
- How can we retain our Northeast Delta Dental culture? A large-scale international survey of workers by Glassdoor's recruiting site revealed that over half of job candidates say that company culture is more important than salary to them. As more of us than before COVID will probably continue to work remotely, this could significantly impact our culture in the future. Our Northeast Delta Dental culture, our commitment to "Healthy Smiles", and our collegiality are vital to our success. We want to make sure we can maintain that while operating with so many people working remotely. Although we have very low turnover among our employees, we worry about how to maintain our quality and our spirit

as people gradually turn over. For instance, since the pandemic, a few people have retired, and one took a great new job; and we are bringing on new employees to replace them. As we do so, in 15 years, if we stay as virtual as we are today, perhaps 20% of our employees will never have worked on campus. What will this mean for our soul?

- Because crises are a time of great stress for everyone, because we want to maintain our culture even when employees work remotely, and because we want to hear what's on our employees' minds in an open and relaxed setting, we are beginning what we call Virtual Talks Around the Water Cooler. One Friday a month at various lunch times via Webex, a Northeast Delta Dental employee will lead a discussion around interesting non-work topics such as music, pets, or vacations. The topic leader will talk for about five minutes, and then there will be 25 more minutes for me and everyone else to join the conversation. Our goal is to hear what is on people's minds, offer encouragement, and maintain the communication and teamwork that are two of our values and are vital to our culture.

- How can we continue to support working mothers and fathers? In many companies, those parents most responsible for their children's remote learning (usually women) were extremely stressed as they tried to work from home while taking care of their children. In other words, working remotely was a huge challenge for many parents, and it's important for Northeast Delta Dental and other employers to be sure our working parents can continue their careers as they wish. Fortunately, we created the Parent Support Group and have always encouraged the mothers and fathers on our staff to maintain a healthy work/life balance. During the pandemic, I personally tried to emphasize that it is fine to spend time with our children by showing photos of my granddaughter, Havanna, and me interacting. We acknowledge that children will inevitably distract parents, that this is fine, and that it is important to be flexible and take care of oneself and one's children. In fact, I get kudos from parents for being so family-oriented. Parents are really happy working here and always have been. Now, they know they can work from home and be supported as they care for their kids. We will be sure we continue on this path.

- Finally, what is the best way to handle the issue of vaccinations? In the early summer of 2021, the Northeast Delta Dental leadership team discussed whether to mandate vaccinations. We ultimately decided to ask, rather than mandate, because, as Jim Schleckser of Inc. CEO Project puts it, "It is tempting to pull rank to drive short-term results, but you'll pay for it in the long run." Instead of ordering vaccinations, we opted to act as role models and advocates for everyone's health. We put personal stories about us getting vaccinated in our newsletters. We encouraged everyone to take care of themselves and their families by getting vaccinated. We publicized and encouraged our employees to take advantage of mass vaccination sites. However, we stopped short of mandating vaccinations, and felt good about that.

The challenge is that, as of this writing, it's difficult to know what the exact rules and interpretations regarding vaccinations will be and whether we can continue to leave the choice to our employees. In September 2021, President Biden directed the Department of Labor's Occupational Safety and Health Administration (OSHA) to issue a rule requiring all businesses with 100 or more employees to ensure their workers are vaccinated and/or tested once a week.

In early November, OSHA issued that rule in the form of a lengthy Emergency Temporary Standard (ETS). This mandated masks for unvaccinated employees effective in December and vaccinations or weekly testing for employees effective in January 2022. Then the U.S. Court of Appeals for the Fifth Circuit stayed the ETS order, but, as of this writing, the U.S. Department of Justice asked the Sixth Circuit to reinstate the ETS. Meanwhile, in New Hampshire, employers also have to keep an eye on a 1951 statute (275:3), which many interpret as requiring New Hampshire employers to pay for the cost of COVID-19 testing. The only thing certain is that Northeast Delta Dental will comply when the rules are clear and will continue to prioritize the health and safety of our employees. My role model for servant leadership, Max De Pree, suggests that a leader should help define realities for employees, so we did our best to explain the OSHA rules and ETS in a November communication which you can find in the Appendix on page 113.

I've concluded that the crisis has accelerated many positive changes, and it is up to us to make sure the changes continue to be for the better by closely monitoring their impact on our people and our culture.

Conclusions

It has now been over one and a half years since the start of the pandemic. Unfortunately, it's too early to say the crisis is over. The COVID Delta variant has increased illnesses, and there is great variation from state to state in infections and COVID's impact on business and society. Business and government leaders are trying to learn how to function in this "new normal" environment.

What actions can leaders take amid a crisis that drags on? As I look ahead, several conclusions stand out for me about leading during this crisis and others. I believe in these conclusions and hope they will help you and other leaders move ahead successfully — to thrive as well as survive, to be resilient, and to bounce forward rather than just bouncing back.

1. Base Crisis Response on Authentic Values

I cannot say strongly enough how important it is to live up to your values and mission — the aspirational goals and motivating forces of an organization — during a crisis. They will trigger you to make the right choices. In our case, our mission of advancing oral health (as summarized in the statement that "Everybody deserves a healthy smile") helped us quickly realize that we needed to support all our stakeholders in working toward this goal. We knew we had to do our best to ensure our employees and participating dentists could do their work and that our customers could get the dental treatments they needed even in an uncertain economy. Since our Boards and Executive Committees knew and supported our mission, they could quickly authorize Northeast Delta Dental and the Northeast Delta Dental Foundation to pay out the $27 million to our stakeholders. As you recall, we used that money to give employees emergency relief time off, dentists relief in the form of reimbursements for masks and gowns as well as more generous claims payment terms, customers premium forgiveness for a month, brokers commissions even when premiums were returned, and donations to community nonprofits so they could carry on their missions.

Our four core values (communication, teamwork, quality, and integrity) also guided our response to the pandemic. We communicated often and honestly with all stakeholders. We worked as a team with our employees, dentists, Boards, and regulators to support our mission. We ensured that the quality of our work and the service provided to our dentists and customers actually improved during the crisis. And we operated with full transparency and integrity. These values and our mission guided us as we balanced our financial support for the community of stakeholders against profits. We did what felt right rather than what would maximize our short run company finances.

I ask myself what would have happened if Northeast Delta Dental had not had such clear mission goals and values? What would have happened if we were not such a values-driven organization? And I conclude that our response would not have been as powerful, timely, or easy to determine without the clarity of our goals.

As you consider your own situation, you also will be in the best position to take action during a crisis if your goals and values are clear. Living up to your values authentically will help you emerge from a crisis strong and proud.

2. Do Well by Doing What's Right

It's possible to emerge from a crisis stronger than ever by doing what's right. We did well on all three of our important measurement dimensions: Operational, Market, and Financial.

Northeast Delta Dental managed to maintain our very high operating standards and employee loyalty during the pandemic.

Operational and Turnover Measures	2019	2020	2021
Average seconds to reach a knowledgeable customer service representative	30	34	23 estimated
Percent of calls resolved in one contact	97%	96%	96%
Abandoned call rate (low is good)	2%	2%	<1%
Percent of dental claims processed within 15 days	99.9%	99.9%	99.9%
Financial accuracy of claims processing	99.95%	100.0%	99.80%
Employee turnover rate (national average is 23%.)	14%	14%	5% (thru July)

Here's a letter we received in early 2021 from a dentist and Northeast Delta Dental Board member praising us for our performance:

> Tom, Those numbers are really impressive! During those few months, the speed in which calls to my payroll company get answered went from about one minute to 2-3 hours. It's wonderful that Northeast Delta Dental has been able to maintain these numbers during a pandemic!

Here's another letter from a subscriber family praising our Customer Service representatives for the quality of their service:

> Dear Tom, We just wanted to say that Northeast Delta Dental customer service exceeded our expectations in helping us to navigate the complexities of insurance. Edwin and Magen have been efficient and timely and, most important, they respond. Thank you for having staff that have the ability to get things done.

Our nearly perfect operations, our financial forgiveness, and our stream of communications to customers and dentists during the pandemic earned Northeast Delta Dental strong customer loyalty as seen in these market measures. We believe our genuine care for our customers during the worst of the pandemic in our states in 2020 helped us retain over 97% of customers and even add new customers. And, in 2021, we are on track to add and retain even more customers.

End of Year Market Measures	2019	2020	2021 (thru June)
Number of new covered lives	48,592	9,070	22,562
Customer retention (industry average is 87%)	98.1%	97.6%	99.1%
Number of participating dentists	1,806	1,858	1,829

Finally, Northeast Delta Dental came out well financially in the end even though we gave away $27 million — or nearly 8% of our revenue for 2020. The chart below compares some of our key financial measures from 2019 before the pandemic with our projected results for 2021 as we emerged from the crisis.

Financial Measures	2019	2020	2021
Operating margin*	.2%	.5%	0%
Mission support to Foundation	$616,279	$404,214	$472,963 YTD

*A word about our operating margin: It shows the percent of our total revenues that we end with net of our claims and operations expenses and before our investment income. In our case, for every $1 we take in as revenue, we pay $.90 to our dentists and then have $.10 for our operating expenses and operating margin. Our ratio of .5% in 2020 means that it cost us $.095 to operate and that we had $.005 or half a cent to retain as our operating margin. We are delighted with this margin because it means we did not lose money or make too much. Even not-for-profits need to avoid losing money and try to make a small amount to hedge against bad years.

But even more than the increase in our financial and market strength, I'm proud of how our reputation grew. As you can see from the letters from stakeholders earlier in Section 2 of this book, we have earned the trust and loyalty of employees, dentists, and customers because we showed them in very tangible ways that we sincerely cared about their well-being. For me, hearing from them and knowing that we helped is perhaps the biggest reward for doing the right thing.

> "Do the right thing, at the right time, for the right reason, and you can't go wrong."

When you face a crisis, based on our experience, you can reassure yourself that investing in doing the right thing for your stakeholders will ultimately make you stronger and happier, too. Paraphrasing Dave Cowens, the outstanding basketball player, civic leader, and co-author of my first book on leadership, I like to say, "Do the right thing, at the right time, for the right reason, and you can't go wrong."

3. Focus on the Long Term

I have learned over four decades that if you pay attention to your people and customers and focus on your long-term vision and mission, then profits take care of themselves quite nicely. Northeast Delta Dental has always been Main Street, not Wall Street: Our not-for-profit corporate structure 501(C)(4) encourages a long-term view without worrying about Wall Street perceptions. This long-term view, embodied by the Baldrige Performance Excellence framework, has been critical to our financial success and growth. This enabled us to give money away to our stakeholders, knowing that helping them succeed would make us more successful.

Of course, giving money away from our reserves would not have been possible if we had not been building them gradually over the years because of the success of our strategic plans. Bestowing money and focusing on the long term is more difficult for firms that are for-profit and answer to investors than for not-for-profits like us. But building reserves and focusing on building long-term market power through customer loyalty will lead to long-term success even if not to short-term profits.

Operating in a secure financial position and having market strength before a crisis hits makes it much easier to weather a disaster when it does happen.

4. Adopt a "Level 5" Servant Leader Style

Some leadership styles work better than others — especially during a crisis. While top-down, authoritative leadership styles may be acceptable in certain situations, I don't believe they work as well as a collaborative style most of the time and certainly don't work well in times of great change.

An article, "Research: Women Are Better Leaders During a Crisis," in the December 30, 2020, *Harvard Business Review*, by Jack Zenger and Joseph Folkman, assessed the leadership effectiveness of women and men leaders before and during the COVID-19 crisis. Not only were women rated more effective than men before the crisis began, but their superiority gap also actually increased during the crisis. Why? The best leaders did four things especially well: 1–Inspire and motivate, 2–Communicate powerfully, 3–Collaborate/use teamwork, and 4–Build relationships. These are all interpersonal skills and require the best leaders to show they are aware of, concerned about, and empathize with their followers' feelings.

This ties in beautifully with my "servant leader" style — seeing my job as putting my employees' welfare first and supporting them so they can perform their best — and the Level 5 leadership criteria on which my personal performance is evaluated. As mentioned earlier, Level 5 refers to the highest level in a hierarchy of executive capabilities identified by the research of Jim Collins and his team. Level 5 Leadership includes personal humility, producing sustained results, concern for the company's success rather than personal recognition or wealth, setting up successors for success, and taking responsibility when things go poorly while attributing success to others.

Of course, a big part of being an effective leader is the ability to communicate with employees, customers, and other stakeholders. I recommend asking yourself these questions to determine whether you will be able to communicate as you should during this and later crises. If you answer no, I suggest that you develop or acquire the communication tools that you need.

1. Do I have the ability to communicate directly with my customers using emails, videos, social media, or other means?
2. If my employees are not able to come into the office, can I reach them effectively through texts, emails, or Zoom/Webex meetings?
3. Have I developed the critical personal skill to show empathy and embrace diversity of background and thought at least as well during Zoom/Webex events as I could in person?

My advice to any leader facing a crisis is to aim to be a Level 5 leader and always go above and beyond what is expected. We went above and beyond the norm of what's expected when we gave away the $27 million in 2020. No one would have criticized us if we had not forgiven our customers' premiums for a month, or if we had not provided free masks and discounted gowns to dentists, or increased our donations to nonprofits. No one would have expected other firms to promise their employees that they would be taken care of. But we at Northeast Delta Dental did make that promise because we wanted to go beyond the expected to the next level of leadership.

And the result of being a Level 5 servant leader who goes above and beyond is that I was able to work with my executives and employees, my Boards, and my other stakeholders during the pandemic to quickly build consensus about how best to weather the crisis. In short, managers who adopt the servant leader style and who aim to be Level 5 will be in the best position to lead their organizations successfully through a crisis.

I must emphasize, however, that being a servant leader doesn't mean neglecting oneself. At the beginning of the pandemic, I was oftentimes spending 16 hours a day at my computer doing emails and Webex/Zoom video conferences. I began to gain weight and found myself suffering from various symptoms of stress, such as vertigo. Eventually, I learned that I had to take care of myself in order to take care of Northeast Delta Dental and its people. I began making time for family and friends and for physical exercise. In the beginning, I walked and ran and then, when it was safe, I went for workouts at Orangetheory Fitness, TITLE Boxing, and Storms Fitness (thank you Cindy Glass and Kelli Cyr). I encouraged everyone at Northeast Delta Dental to take a wellness break and engage in some form of physical activity, with the help of our Northeast Delta Dental fitness coach, Tom Walton.

I love to run and was very fortunate that John Mortimer and the Millennium Running Team developed COVID-safe guidelines for running road races that were approved by New Hampshire Governor Sununu's Re-Opening Task Force. So, I ran as many races as I could and encouraged others to do the same because I found running boosted my mental as well as physical health. As I regained my health, I found I was able to do a better job of leading. So, do please take care of yourself so you can do your best as a leader.

5. Build Trust

Trust pays off whether there is a crisis or not. A May 2021 study by Deloitte found that customers who trust a company are more likely to try a new product or service offered by that company than by a less-trusted company: "Lacking trust can be expensive." Similarly, employees who trust their companies are more likely to want to continue working for their companies. A 2017 *Harvard Business Review* article by Paul Zak, "The Neuroscience of Trust," showed that employees at trusted companies have significantly less stress, higher productivity, more energy at work, fewer sick days, more engagement, more satisfaction in their lives, and less burnout.

An August 2021 survey from PricewaterhouseCoopers highlighted the importance of trust. It said that organizations are "facing two critical challenges at once: retaining employees and leading the charge on making hybrid work a success. First, there's the great 'employee exodus' with 65% of employees saying they're looking for a new job ... Second, there's the new world of hybrid work and ... the risk of remote work inequity." As I read this, my takeaway is that it's more important than ever that employees feel valued and genuinely like and trust their leaders.

So how can a leader build trust? Jack Zenger and Joseph Folkman wrote in 2019 on "The Three Elements of Trust" in *Harvard Business Review* that their research showed that leaders who were judged a bit above average in consistency, in good judgment, and in positive relationships earned trust that was well above average. An opinion piece by George Shultz at age 100 in the December 11, 2020, *Washington*

Post echoed that thought: "Often in my career, I saw that genuine empathy is essential in establishing solid, trusting relationships." In a March 25, 2021, blog post on Blogrige, Harry Hertz, "The Baldrige Cheermudgeon," wrote on "Regaining Trust: Lead with Facts, Listen and Act with Empathy." He said that trust begins with the facts and the only way to recover from lost trust is with honesty.

I've tried to earn trust by delivering on all the commitments I make. I like to say I underpromise and overdeliver. The Northeast Delta Dental Guarantee Of Service Excellence℠ (GOSE℠) is a great example. We promise to meet several goals, and if we don't, we "turn ourselves in" to our customers. We don't wait for them to notice and ask for the penalty payments. Instead, we keep track of our performance and make good on our promises, fulfilling our pledges proactively. This impresses our customers and also impressed John Tschohl, author of *Relentless*, who wrote about our GOSE℠ exemplary service and relentless commitment to our customers.

Another example is how we built trust with our employees during the pandemic. We were candid from the beginning of the crisis that we couldn't guarantee to bring everyone back but that we would try our best. In the end, we succeeded. We had to lay off only two out of our 200+ employees, and those laid off were people who planned or attended in-person events which were no longer held. They understood the situation, were given a generous exit package, and knew that they left with strong reputations and our thanks. We also told employees as the pandemic was ending that we would allow everyone who was working remotely to continue to do so if they wished. Out of the 150 or so who were virtual, only 50 have opted to come back in person, and those who prefer to work remotely have had their wishes respected.

For our dentists, we told them we would help them stay in business. We gave them $7 million, we supplied them with subsidized gowns and with masks that were initially free and later discounted, and we promoted teledentistry. Our commitment to honoring our promises to dentists is one of the reasons why Northeast Delta Dental has one of the best relationships with its dentists in the association of Delta Dental Plans Member Companies.

I was pleased to read Professor Leonard Berry and Dr. Rana Awdish's 2021 article about the importance of creating a generous and trusting culture in order to excel. They say, "being generous with employees strengthens their sense of community, security, loyalty, and trust and inspires them to go the extra mile to serve others. That discretionary effort — the difference between the effort workers *voluntarily* expend versus what they *must* expend to avoid penalty — is critical to the success of all service organizations ... However, strengthening a culture is difficult and slow. To start, leaders must narrow any trust gap between them and employees by always being truthful, promoting transparency, listening actively, practicing inclusion over exclusion, investing in the benefits that matter the most, and being visible."

As they recommend, we have worked hard at Northeast Delta Dental to earn trust before the crisis and to maintain it with honest communications and caring actions during the crisis. This has inspired our employees and has added to our company's reputation. And, if you work to earn trust, you, too, will earn the loyalty of your stakeholders before, during, and after a crisis.

6. Embrace the Proven Baldrige Principles

Because of the enormous payoff we have had from Baldrige Performance Excellence Program principles, I always advise other leaders to embrace this tried and tested model. Looking back, we did several things that helped us succeed with the Baldrige model, and I share them in the hopes of making others' journeys equally successful.

1. **Take the time to really understand the criteria.** I did it by taking the Baldrige examiner training, and I honestly believe that the few weeks this takes delivers at least as much wisdom as two years of business school. Northeast Delta Dental's most enthusiastic ambassadors are those employees who completed examiner training, whether they took it at the state or national level or whether they ever examined another company or not.
2. **Share the learning with others in your organization.** Having Northeast Delta Dental's top leaders also take examiner training created a solid team of ambassadors or apostles. They not only supported our efforts but expanded the ideas and outcomes through their wisdom.
3. **Start with early wins for your organization.** Change, like a diet, requires one to have a goal in mind and stick to the plan. This is not easy, and it's possible for the efforts to become just another forgotten New Year's

resolution or idea of the month. We started with improved efficiency and quality through defining and managing our work processes. This had immediate payoffs. We followed with the focus on the customer service guarantee because this produced results quickly.

4. **Persuade key stakeholders to support the effort.** We had to persuade both the Board and the employees. We did this by highlighting the early wins and by having lots of measures to prove that we were improving.
5. **Always focus on doing what's right** — for employees, for customers, for society. If you do this, the results will come.
6. **Leadership must have an unwavering commitment to excellence.** Sustained change based on the Baldrige model and values requires a fanatical focus by leaders. To successfully implement Baldrige as we did first at Delta Dental of Massachusetts and then at Northeast Delta Dental, the commitment must come from the top, from leaders who lead by example. Success cannot be delegated.
7. **Baldrige can work for any kind of organization.** The Baldrige framework and its core values apply to any size organization in any type of industry. I feel confident Baldrige can work for your organization as it did for mine.

As I wrote for the Baldrige Foundation Institute for Performance Excellence, "I believe that if you take care of your customers and your people, the results will take care of themselves. If people are happy at work, they will deliver great service and be recognized and rewarded. If customers are happy, they will remain loyal and tell others, increasing sales and revenues. And if operations are efficient and error-free, they will save money. It's a beautiful circle, where paying attention to your people leads to customer loyalty, which leads to great results."

7. Be Ready for the Next Disaster

In April 2021, the Committee for Economic Development of The Conference Board issued a new report in its series on *Sustaining Capitalism*. It stressed that there will be future pandemics and that failure to master the lessons learned from the COVID-19 pandemic — including the vital role played by the business community — could be catastrophic. No matter how well managed an organization may be, no one is immune from the uncontrollable. Therefore, every organization — no matter its size or industry — should have a disaster recovery plan. Without it, valuable time, resources, and even lives will be lost. One way to start developing your disaster recovery plan is to study the 2021-2022 Baldrige Excellence Framework's discussion of resiliency and the importance of planning to protect your employees, customers, society, and financial well-being.

Many predict that the next crisis will relate to cybersecurity as our dependence on technology, whether working from home or the office, grows and greatly increases our exposure and risk. Regardless of the cause, it is vital to have up-to-date crisis recovery plans.

And just because organizations have disaster recovery plans for all the possible external threats (weather or other natural disasters; fires, bombs, or explosions; power and equipment failures; nuclear, biological, or chemical accidents; intruders; suspicious packages; and pandemics), they are not home free. We at Northeast Delta Dental have a proactive Pandemic/Disaster Recovery Team that meets regularly to ask, "What could go wrong?"

As part of Northeast Delta Dental's efforts to keep our disaster recovery plans up to date and robust, we conduct periodic exercises to test our plans, documentation, and ability to restore our functioning. In our case, we conducted our test in April 2021. Our goal was to complete the exercise in 16 hours, and we were pleased that it only took a bit over ten hours. However, we found that we needed over 20 improvements to our written guides and over 10 technical issue improvements! So, even though we were still living through the COVID disaster and had detailed plans for responding, our test showed us that we needed to do even more work to have truly robust plans.

To determine your need for a thorough and up-to-date disaster recovery plan, I recommend asking yourself these questions. And, if the answer to them is no, then please think about taking action.

1. Do I have a written disaster recovery plan that helps my organization deal with the COVID crisis and others that may come?
2. If I have a plan, has it been updated and tested through simulation each year?
3. Do I have a designated team that will implement the plan when needed and will monitor relevant government policies and directives?

When a crisis hits, it is important to recognize its arrival. To again paraphrase Bill Gates and other visionaries, crises and trends are obvious in the rear-view mirror but may be difficult to recognize when looking ahead. So, what can we all do? First look for signs, such as the ones I was slow to spot when the NBA canceled its season or people began wearing masks. Also, listen when someone you trust raises a concern. In my case, it was Delta Dental Plan of Maine Board member Bruce Nickerson who asked if we should meet in person in March 2020.

Finally, it's essential to have a tolerance for ambiguity or uncertainty when responding to a crisis. We must accept — even if we are not comfortable doing so — that we are making the best decisions possible with our current information, and then we have to be willing to adapt those decisions when we have more data.

8. Most Importantly, Strengthen the Foundation

In the first section of this book, I talked about the importance of having a strong foundation in order to be prepared to face a crisis. In the second section, I talked about how Northeast Delta Dental responded to the crisis, building on our strong foundational elements. Now, as I look ahead to the inevitable future disasters, my main recommendation is to continue to learn from our experiences during this crisis, maintaining and strengthening our foundations.

As I wrote to employees in May 2021, "As we begin to emerge from the pandemic, please think about the muscle memory you developed during the darker days of the pandemic, your new virtual competencies, resiliency, and your elimination of work activities that don't deliver value. We'll need those skill sets and learnings to be used post-pandemic. It's also okay to be unconventional at times. Some of the best innovations in human history have occurred when the inventor was being unconventional, trying something new, or getting out of her or his comfort zone."

How can we all strengthen our foundations for the future?

- Find the right balance between the efficiency and desirability of remote work and the need for the face-to-face personal connections that develop future leaders and maintain the best cultural values.
- Continue to work on understanding the needs of all stakeholders and on communicating with and listening to them. This is especially important as more and more of our interactions are virtual.

- Invest in and expand the technology developed during the pandemic, while making sure that the new work processes are high quality, quick, easy to perform, and error-free. I recommend that you regularly review your organization's cybersecurity precautions, the strength of your IT technology, and the availability of all technology and equipment that your employees need to access during crises.
- Use Baldrige performance excellence principles and performance measurement to identify where improvements and innovations are needed.
- Keep growing financial reserves while investing in ways to increase diversity, equity, and inclusion in human resources, in the services or products provided, and in support for our communities.
- Above all, remain true to the vision, mission, and values of the organization. And practice honesty and build trust in all communications.

What If It's Not Over? What If We Face Other Disasters?

When I started writing this book in 2020, I envisioned that the COVID crisis would have an end, we would vanquish the virus, and we would return to work more or less as normal. That has not proven to be the case.

As I write this book, the country is still in the midst of the COVID crisis. Dr. Mark McClellan (former FDA Commissioner and Director, Duke-Robert J. Margolis Center for Health Policy) spoke to the Conference Board's Committee for Economic Development in July of 2021 and stressed that the COVID Delta variant is aggressive and much more dangerous than other versions. While vaccinations and boosters help, and the military, other governmental agencies, healthcare organizations, and many employers are requiring vaccinations in all but a few rare exceptions, the pandemic continues. With the emergence of the Omicron variant, Dr. McClellan and many public health experts believe that the crisis is far from over.

John Kay and Mervyn King, in their excellent 2020 book, *Radical Uncertainty*, talk about the importance of making decisions in an "unknowable future". Similarly, Bill Koenigsberg, CEO of Horizon Media, says, "There will be no such thing as a post-pandemic landscape that settles into some predictable new picture." He adds that business leaders must accept the reality of continued uncertainty to "move our companies forward through a fog that isn't going to lift." They and I believe that the best way to move forward is to accept the complexity and uncertainty we face and use a multidimensional, systems-thinking approach to decision making.

Even if we are eventually successful in taming COVID so it is just another flu, many experts tell us that there will be other pandemics. Also, we may be affected by natural disasters, which seem to be growing in number and severity. And let's not overlook the very real cybersecurity risks organizations of all types and sizes face.

So, what if we face the real risk of a new disasters? My conclusion is that it's more important than ever to be prepared and that it's never too late to start. Everything we have learned about managing during a crisis still applies — maybe more so than if the crisis were behind us. We all must work to build and maintain the kind of strong foundations that will let us survive and even thrive during the crisis. That involves many things:

- Being the best leaders we can be personally
- Knowing our employees, customers, competitors, and our own strengths and weaknesses
- Having a mission, vision, and core values to guide and motivate everyone in our organization to do what's right
- Using best governance practices for our Boards of Directors and daily management
- Having robust strategic plans that focus on long-term success and include specific plans for managing disasters
- Insisting on performance excellence in our daily work and operations
- Building a strong and motivated workforce, investing in and safeguarding our technologies, and having sufficient financial reserves to make it through a crisis

Early readers of this book told me they planned to keep it on their bookshelves and re-read it when faced with their next crisis. I don't like to be pessimistic, but more recent readers of this book say they believe it is so indispensable — given the environment we face today — that they'll keep it right on their desks or bedside tables. No matter where you keep your copy, I hope you are able to adapt many of its ideas to your situation.

Questions About Where to Start

1. What if your organization is in the midst of the COVID or other crisis, and you still haven't built a strong foundation? Where can you start?

    Thought 1: It's never too late to start, so why not start with yourself? How do you consider your effectiveness as a leader? Could you become a servant leader? If so, where might you change to achieve that style? If not, could you consider ways to improve your communications and relationships with your employees and other stakeholders?

    Thought 2: You always need to budget. You still need to spend on salaries, safety, equipment, raw materials, and other purchases. Can you think of these expenditures as investments in your future? Can your budget include saving or building a financial cushion to help fund these investments?

2. Of all aspects of your organization, which ones are helping you build the resiliency you need to survive the crisis? Which ones make you lose sleep at night? What can you do to address those?

    Another thought: During the crisis, many of us find we are spending a great deal of alone time in front of our computers each day. Travel and meeting times have been greatly reduced. This "found time" is actually an ideal time to plan and envision the future as you would like it to be. Why not use this time to consider how to build your organization's foundation in ways that would strengthen your reputation, operational quality, and market position? What actions can help your organization thrive as well as survive?

3. What is your vision for your organization? Which of the recommendations in this section would help you achieve that vision?

4. How can you recruit and motivate others to work with you on changes to strengthen your organization?

5. Are you prepared to acknowledge and deal with people's emotions when they return to the office — or when they can't? These emotions are real, as I've experienced myself when seeing people again for the first time in over a year.

6. If you have 100 or more employees in your organization, have you studied the OSHA Emergency Temporary Standard (ETS) and other relevant guidelines? While it remains to be seen if the ETS will stick or not, are you prepared and ready to implement the new required processes? Just as importantly, have you communicated with your employees about the new ETS and guidelines? Do you have a pulse on how your employees are feeling about these new rules? Have you had roundtable discussions (virtual or otherwise) on this topic with employees? Are you prepared for the potential loss of employees over the implementation of the ETS?

Communications Appendix

Sample Communications to Each Stakeholder Group

To Employees

My first communications were with our employees. My goal was to reassure them that their safety came first and to let them know what to expect. We delayed furloughs as long as we could but then sent this communication to those employees who had to be furloughed:

First Email to Furloughed Employees

April 9, 2020

Good Thursday Evening Professional Colleagues,

I know this a challenging time for all of us, and I'm sorry that I was not personally involved with your meetings with Connie, or could not dialogue with you individually due to time constraints, and not lack of concern or caring. Suffice to say though, I've been involved with Connie every step of the way, as we attempted to be as flexible as possible with the emergency time off, then limit furloughs to when they became necessary because of lack of work activities as so few people can go to the dentist (emergency treatment only) and many dental offices have closed down completely for now.

I do believe that there is light at the end of this COVID-19 tunnel, that dentists — albeit in a measured way with enhanced infection control guidelines — will see patients again for regular procedures, and that we will return to a former level of dental activity, though I think it will be more measured for patients too, as they won't be rushing back, and dentists will follow a modified workflow.

Northeast Delta Dental is taking all strategic steps to be ready for the post COVID-19 dental space recovery, and we have attempted to be as generous and fair as possible to employees, our dentists through relief efforts, our group purchasers who are struggling financially and going through layoffs, and individual citizen customers who have been granted flexibility to step off their DeltaDentalCoversMe.com plan, but with an ability to come back without penalty.

I will stay in touch with you via this Listserv/email grouping regularly. In accordance with Company Information security protocols and to be sure we don't put your potential unemployment benefits in jeopardy, please do not reach out to Northeast Delta Dental/csONE/PreViser employees with work questions. I know this is a challenge because they are your work family and friends. In the spirit of transparency, I have let all colleagues know the names of the 15-16% of our workforce who have been furloughed, and I know they feel the same sense of empathy and loss as I do that, for now, you are no longer actively employed. To quote one colleague: "We are in solidarity with those who are not employed."

We will get through this. Together We Can (TWC). Please use this time to deepen connections with your family and other loved ones, stay physically healthy, and as mentioned in a previous communication, do something you have dreamed of doing for a while, but never had the time.

Take great care. I will be back in touch.

Typical Daily Email — One of Nearly 400 Sent from March 2020 through October 2021

We now know that the pandemic is not going to suddenly end and that we will have to continue our vigilance. This short email is typical of those I sent almost every weekday to thank and encourage all our dedicated and valued employees:

September 18, 2021

Good Friday Morning Colleagues,

Another week almost in the books. As I made the rounds on Thursday, colleagues on campus look energized and healthy. Thank you on campus employee colleagues. Virtual employee colleagues who also connect with me, I know, are continuing their wellness/fitness breaks. Thank you virtual employee colleagues. And please remember to record your exercise in the fitness log so we can reimburse you.

I am also appreciative that colleagues are being safe and responsible, with masks (example attached, first photo) and social distancing. I think this is going to be our way of life for a few years, so I am proud and happy that we continue to thrive, while respecting the virus.

Tom W's tidbit is in green below, concerning bone and muscle strength and coordination. The Two Delta Fitness Center soft re-opening this week went well; thank you Tom W and thanks on-campus colleagues following guidelines. Speaking of Tom W, he was recently named to the NHTI Athletics Hall of Fame, recognizing his exemplary work leading the NHTI cross-country team for many years. I know you join me in congratulating Coach Tom W.

Please enjoy your weekend ahead.

This was sent at the end of 2020 as an update on our very encouraging recovery process:

End of Year Email to Employees

December 10, 2020

Good Thursday Morning Colleagues,

Yesterday's DDPVT Board Meeting was both efficient and effective, with Zoom technology flawless, and with all Budget and SMART Goal motions passing unanimously, quickly, and enthusiastically. This completes the trifecta of State Board meetings (DDPME, DDPNH, and now DDPVT) so we are all set for 2021! Next week we do have short meetings with the PreViser Board and our Common Subsidiary Board to review csONE and PreViser results. We anticipate that these meetings will also be smooth. The State Boards are pleased with the work of all our family of companies, csONE, PreViser, and Northeast Delta Dental. And DDPVT Board Chair, Dr. David Solomon, and all Board members really, extend their thanks to you, all colleagues, for your dedication, especially in this unusual and challenging 2020.

The photo gallery continues today, with pictures of other poinsettias which can be seen at the One and Two Delta campuses, and Sara has provided the Holiday décor in the Executive area.

It was Harry's birthday yesterday (12/9 – card is coming Harry), so we trust Mr. Pike had a nice day with his family.

Please remember the Humanities Presentation, today at noon (please see Christina's emails on this; really cool on dog sledding, and I know Laurie B will be joining the show), and to say your fond farewells to our esteemed GC, Erica Bodwell.

Tom W's lexicon lesson continues below in green and red. Please make it a great Thursday. Pretty mild in NH for December, so a nice day for a walk break. TWC.

Coach Tom R

In early 2021, I was able to tell employees that Northeast Delta Dental was doing well enough to resume pension payments:

Email about Pension Payments

March 25, 2021

Good Morning Amazing Colleagues,

I trust Northeast Delta Dental colleagues checked your bank accounts this morning (hopefully not at 1:18 am when my notification arrived). Thank you, Bonnie, for your precise payroll expertise (Bonnie is our PPE). Speaking of PPE (as in Personal Protection Equipment), a major shipment of nitrile gloves arrived yesterday, and Laureen will be shipping out supplies of gloves to our participating dentists in need, who pay for them on a discounted basis. In this way, we ensure that dental offices remain open.

One quick note as I have been asked about this by a few colleagues — this year, in addition to the 3% safe harbor contribution to your Retirement account (which will be coming up soon), we will also add another 2% to the Discretionary plan, so you will (if eligible, and that is most everyone) receive a roughly 5% contribution to your Retirement account. Last year at this time, given the uncertainty, I asked our Board to allow us to take the Discretionary percentage and transition that into a second cash bonus. This year, we know that while some challenges still exist with COVID-19 (we are still not at the finish line), we believe — as I have noted many times — that our future and our dental industry is bright. Given that, and because we really encourage people to save for Retirement (it sneaks up on you), we are keeping the second contribution as an add to the Retirement account, and not cash. Thanks for understanding this and thank you for keeping your retirement planning in mind, and I'm glad so many of you have been dialoguing with our new pension advisor team (FSRP, led by Shawn Monty), who have the same degree of expertise and caring as Dennis Lynch had (Dennis, btw, is happy in retirement in Florida).

I sent this email to employees to summarize the amazing progress they and Northeast Delta Dental had made in the year of the COVID:

First Year Update Email

March 24, 2021

Hi Colleagues,

As promised, the second Happy email for Wednesday:

We've been through an extraordinary year in 2020 — and we did it together. We're pleased you're a member of the Northeast Delta Dental/csONE/PreViser team and despite all the challenges 2020 brought, we have good news to share with you about our SMART Goals and other important accomplishments we completed!

We ended 2020 with a 99.5% combined ratio (Friendly Frank was smiling)! We appreciate our Finance and Actuarial and Underwriting experts who analyze data and crunch the numbers to assure we balance the books and price our products correctly and precisely!

In spite of the pandemic, our Sales and Account Management team added 28,610 new primary dental subscribers in 2020, reaching 93% of the annual sales goal. Through January of this year, we now cover more than 960,000 lives under our dental plans (marching to a million!). In addition, the team added nearly 4,000 new DeltaVision® subscribers, achieving 133% of the annual sales goal!

In addition to this great news, we also retained 98.1% of our group customers (including our three state accounts) in 2020. Considering the industry average is 87%, 98% is truly remarkable. Northeast Delta Dental has three of the top five customer retention rates in the entire Delta Dental system, including spots one and two. Remember, customers renew when they are highly satisfied with a company's products and customer service. Kudos to all of you for keeping our customers happy and making it possible for our Account Executives to renew business.

Three other key measures are also on the rise: The growth of our PPO network, the number of customers electing standalone PPO coverage, and the increase in customers with no prior dental coverage (this one is, as you know, mission sensitive)!

Also supporting mission-sensitive work, in 2020 the Northeast Delta Dental Foundation funded 44 oral health programs throughout Maine, New Hampshire, and Vermont. More than $400,000 supported school-based screening and educational programs, nonprofit dental clinics, and workforce development efforts to improve the oral health of people living in our three states.

In an effort to further support our communities, we allowed the organizations to keep the funds even if their program was put on hold due to COVID-19, such as the school-based programs. We also continued our investment to our communities by supporting local social services, arts, educational, and cultural organizations. Our annual golf tournament raises funds for the Foundation. Although the tournament was canceled in 2020, the Foundation still received extra support from the sale of PPE to our participating dentists. That's a win-win!

Despite a very challenging year, the PreViser team met its 2020 Business plan by primarily focusing on 1) retaining existing customers 2) pragmatic expense management and 3) continued improvements and support of the PreViser platform with emphasis on improvements in user experience and onboarding a digital platform. We are looking forward to 2021 and will focus on three key pillars: 1) New Insurance Customers 2) Get traction in NEW revenue opportunities such as DSO Markets, Product Companies (Philips or Colgate) or New innovative partnerships (Tele-Dentistry / AI Technology) and 3) Incremental Improvements of the PreViser Platform to continue to get broader adoption by both dental offices and insurance carriers.

Our Information Systems Team continues our commitment to Agile with a goal to "Deliver Quality Business Solutions Faster." Delivery of changes to our systems is now a biweekly occurrence, and we have reduced the requirement for days of testing down to minutes. The learning and improving continues! On the cybersecurity front, we continue to protect our systems and data by incorporating tests and phishing campaigns designed to help you remain vigilant about the importance of security with our systems and data.

Kudos to Operations teammates working collaboratively to help us achieve our SMART Goals. We met the goal of implementing a new Digital Distribution System for the sale of new small groups. Producers can now shop for dental and vision plans for their clients representing 100 or less subscribers on the new web-based platform. Features include the ability to compare, quote, and initiate a purchase. Further, we implemented a feature that allows for the presentation of renewals to these Producers for the groups purchased through the site.

And thank you to all our Operations colleagues who set up the benefits, enroll subscribers and family members, process and review claims, work with our providers, taught customers how to use Benefit Look-up, and answer the hundreds of thousands of calls from groups, patients, and dentists.

As with other Divisions in the Company, 2020 was a challenging time for the Professional Relations Department, as they successfully transitioned all of their processes to a work-at-home environment. All of this was accomplished with a smaller staff than normal as the slowing of the claims coming into Delta Dental reduced to a dribble during the dental shutdown in March 2020. Even with this disruption, the team continued to meet its metrics and its mission. They continued to nurture relationships with providers and educate the provider community utilizing virtual tools. They continued to review claims and reconsiderations in a timely fashion, and they continued to build on the strong relationships with the dental community that powers a part of the strongly differentiated value proposition that Northeast Delta Dental enjoys in our marketplaces.

The Legal and Compliance Team continues to oversee government relations, federal and state advocacy, risk management, all corporate and regulatory filings, enterprise compliance, and contracts and agreements. Highlights for 2020 include taking a leadership role in the company's pandemic response, coordinating the company's Delta Dental Plans Association audit response, and supporting company responses to state regulatory audits, SOC2 audit, and annual audits, and obtaining Red Tree Insurance Company's license to offer vision insurance in Vermont. Throughout the year, the team continued its advocacy in Maine and New Hampshire for a Medicaid adult dental benefit as well as compliance training and vendor management programs. The team completed its work despite significant staff turnover.

As Benantonio shared at the All Employees Meeting on March 4, csONE's business model continuously evolved in 2020 with a consistent focus on offering effective benefit solutions to meet the dynamic needs of the industry. The 2020 financial results produced a gain before taxes and management fees of over $757,397 versus the full-year budget of $342,379 (221% of the budgeted goal), signaling a tremendous year at csONE Benefit Solutions. After successfully navigating through a rapidly changing marketplace in 2020, csONE is poised for another dynamic year in 2021.

And finally, we're proud to say that after being selected as one of New Hampshire's best companies to work for, Northeast Delta Dental was a Hall of Fame Company in 2020, in the Best Company to Work for in NH competition established by Business NH Magazine. This is testament to our commitment to employee engagement and satisfaction!

In spite of a furlough in April when dental offices closed reducing the number of claims and calls, we were able to bring employees back to work as dental office activity began to increase.

Last year, we welcomed nine new Northeast Delta Dental, csONE employees and our turnover rate of 13.87% was below the national average of 22.8%. We were pleased to return most of our employees from furloughs, some retired, a small number did not return as a result of some reorganizing. We were pleased to be able to provide a safety net of benefits and leave time for employees, keeping everyone in the workplace safe from illness. Employees working remotely received the training and support necessary to successfully work at home — and we're pleased the desks, chairs, and other equipment is keeping you ergonomically safe and healthy. And the Corporate Services team was a great help in making sure our facilities are cleaned and sanitized by increasing disinfecting procedures as part of the daily cleaning process of all high touch areas. Additionally, electronic ionization filters, i-Wave units, were installed in both facilities that eliminate 99.4% of unhealthy pathogens, viruses, irritants, and unwanted odors in the air — including the COVID-19 virus. Not only does it purify the air, but it also eliminates pathogens and viruses on hard nonporous surfaces as well.

Employee development continues to be a company priority, and the Human Resources Team facilitated leadership, management, social justice, technology, wellness, and other programs for your benefit! And let's celebrate — a minor decrease in the cost of our health insurance premiums.

Last year's incidents around the country related to Racial Equity made it clear that Northeast Delta Dental, as members of the community and as good corporate citizens, had an obligation to address these social justice and racial equity issues in some way. A group of leaders was assembled and given the charge of identifying some actions to take. I am proud to share with you that the actions that are being worked on are: Bringing diversity to our governing Boards, bringing education and facilitating discussions about racial equity to the employees, and developing an approach to improving oral health outcomes specifically for communities that are the victims of racial inequities that drive oral health inequity.

In recognition of what we achieved in 2020, our Board of Directors/Trustees have generously supported the annual Team Bonus (paid earlier for csONE and PreViser colleagues, and Thursday, 3/25 for Northeast Delta Dental colleagues) as well as the additional contribution to our retirement plan which will be made in the next few weeks — more details to come soon!

Thank you for your dedication to quality, customer service, and continuous improvement on behalf of Northeast Delta Dental, csONE, and PreViser! And thank you for your loyalty and hard work! We're looking forward to a successful 2021 and appreciate YOU as part of the team!

This November 17, 2021 Communication (number 401 since the pandemic) — as this book literally goes to press — talks about our special award program for exemplary service and loyalty:

> Good Wednesday Morning Amazing Colleagues,
>
> On behalf of the Senior Management Team, I would like to thank you for your years of dedicated service and loyalty to Northeast Delta Dental, csONE, and PreViser!
>
> Our growth, customer retention and satisfaction, and overall success depend on devoted and capable team members (that's you!), and we want to recognize your contributions to achieving our goals!
>
> We celebrate your service with us by sharing a sincere thank you, and also by providing you an award for your tenure with the Company — $5 for each month of service up to a maximum of $1,000 which you will receive, along with your paycheck, on November 18.
>
> I am in awe of the many seasoned employees who provide historical knowledge, wisdom, and mentorship of our less experienced colleagues. Thank you for helping reduce the learning curve for our newer staff members, who appreciate your guidance and support.
>
> In the last twelve months, we warmly welcomed 12 new employee colleagues into our three companies. A little over half of our employee colleagues — 53% to be exact — have been here for 10+ years. A subset of that number, 27% of our employees, have been here for 20+ years. This mix of experience is a great way we continue to foster a culture where everyone continues to develop and improve!
>
> And we warmly welcome our newer employees who bring in new ideas and different ways of thinking. The background you bring based on your external experiences help spark new strategies and tactics as we continue to improve processes and methodologies at Northeast Delta Dental. We encourage you to continue to question "the way things are done" to inspire more imaginative approaches at Northeast Delta Dental, csONE, and PreViser.
>
> We also appreciate the diversity we have in our workforce! More diversity equals more creativity and innovation, and encourages new ways of thinking and

solving problems. We applaud the various perspective each one of you brings to the workplace, and we're proud of our inclusive environment providing equal rights and opportunities for all — regardless of gender, color, nationality, age, ethnicity, physical ability, sexual orientation, religious beliefs, and so on.

As your Coach, I am grateful you're on the team, and I wish you and yours a very Happy Thanksgiving holiday next week. Enjoy a relaxing four-day weekend, and thank you for all you do to contribute to our success.

And two representative responses from employee colleagues:

Thank you Tom, I remember my first service check. It was $15 and I thought "how cool" and still is 31 years later. I hope you have a wonderful Thanksgiving as well.

• • •

Hi Tom: This is a wonderful message. Thank you. I am grateful for the passion that I see in my peers in IS and on my team Kearsarge. That passion can sometimes be found in unexpected ways.

This next employee communication from mid-November 2021 was my effort to describe the realities of the OSHA emergency temporary standard (ETS). (A thank you to Rod Young, President & CEO of Delta Dental of Minnesota, for sharing the mantra, Together We Can, or TWC.)

When you receive an extra communication from me, it's usually very important, but dry. This email you should read very carefully.

On November 5, 2021, the Occupational Safety and Health Administration (OSHA) issued its long-awaited emergency temporary standard (ETS) implementing the federal "vaccine mandate." The ETS requires all private employers with 100 or more workers to ensure all on-site employees are either fully vaccinated for COVID-19, or provide a weekly negative test and wear a face covering while working. Northeast Delta Dental is subject to the ETS.

Those of you who follow the news know that the ETS was immediately challenged in court, and that enforcement of the ETS has been put on hold while the challenge is reviewed. We don't know how or when courts will rule on the ETS. In the meantime, we need to prepare for the ETS as if it will go into effect.

This means that we are actively preparing practices and policies to comply with the ETS. We are planning to implement these policies by January 4, 2022, as required under the ETS. For those of you who are vaccinated and have already provided proof of vaccination to Human Resources, nothing will change.

If, however, you are not fully vaccinated by January 4 for any reason, including medical or religious reasons, and you work on campus — even if only one day a week, you will be required to provide a negative COVID-19 test each week, potentially at your own expense. You will also be required to wear a mask when in the office, except in limited circumstances. We are developing policies around testing and masking for unvaccinated employees who are on campus. We will be announcing these policies and providing training for managers on them in the coming weeks.

If you are not yet vaccinated, we strongly encourage you to get vaccinated as soon as possible. Remember that two of the vaccines, Pfizer and Moderna, require two doses, separated by three and four weeks respectively. And you are not considered "fully vaccinated" under the ETS until two weeks after receiving the second dose (or two weeks after receiving one Johnson & Johnson dose). So it is best to get started now on the vaccination process, even if implementation of the ETS seems a long way off. You can use Earned Time to get vaccinated and/or if you are unable to work due to side effects from the vaccine. The ETS does not require booster shots.

If you have questions about getting vaccinated, the Centers for Disease Control and Prevention has published the attached document to answer many of your questions. You can also ask your doctor if you have specific concerns.

If you are already vaccinated, that is great! If you plan on being in the office, even only sometimes, and you haven't yet sent proof of your vaccination to HR (in the form of a scan or picture of your CDC vaccination card, or record from a medical provider or pharmacy), please do so. Know that these records will be kept secure and confidential, and will only be retained for the duration of the ETS, which will initially be for a period of six months, although it may be renewed.

While I understand that not all employee colleagues will agree with these new policies, Northeast Delta Dental has an obligation to comply with OSHA standards or face stiff penalties for noncompliance. Together, we have done a great job of weathering the pandemic storm. We have already taken a number of steps now required by OSHA, but we will be adding further policies and procedures as necessary to comply with the ETS — all with the goal of maintaining a safe work environment for all colleagues. More to come.

Together We Can. (TWC).
Coach Tom R.

This email from later in November updated my thoughts on health policies:

Good Friday Morning Amazing Colleagues,

I'd like to start this Friday with some good news, and that is, starting Monday, we will no longer require unvaccinated employees to email the daily COVID-19 form to Human Resources. At the very least, this should be good news for Christina. These forms are no longer required by the State, and by this point I hope everyone realizes that if you are not feeling well or if you are exhibiting COVID-19 symptoms, you should not come into the office. Removing this requirement doesn't change the need to stay home if you have symptoms, but it should make the days a little easier for some of us.

I have also received some feedback — both positive and negative — from my Wednesday email regarding the OSHA vaccine mandate. I appreciate hearing all of your thoughts. Communication is one of our core values and it's great that you are embracing that value by reaching out to me. At the same time, I wouldn't be living up to that value if I didn't communicate to you the status of the mandate (currently suspended by OSHA pending review in court) and our plans to comply with the mandate if and when it becomes effective.

With Thanksgiving next week, the holiday season is kicking off. Like many of you, I am disappointed that we will be missing out on our company holiday party for the second year in a row. But I do hope that all of you enjoy your gift cards, whichever one you chose (I chose Common Man), and I understand that the Employee Appreciation Committee is planning a fun virtual holiday party similar to the one which wrapped up Halloween week.

I also understand if some teams or groups of employees miss the personal connection and want to organize their own holiday gatherings, like Yankee swaps or cookie swaps. If any team wishes to do something like this on a voluntary basis, the company won't stand in your way. Given the current COVID-19 situation, we as a company cannot host every employee and their guest at a large event, but we trust you to be responsible if you choose to do something as a small group. If you do, please remember to be safe, masking and maintaining safe distances when appropriate.

In response to my communications about COVID safety, I received these two notes from employees:

Tom,

Just communicating...I am VERY thankful that you and our management team have done such a fantastic job of handling the safety logistics during the pandemic. I am also thankful that you have taken employee safety so seriously.

In the conditions of this pandemic, I have no problems dealing with some cautionary inconveniences and I applaud our team. Thank you so much.

• • •

Good morning Coach Tom! Thank you for this email. More importantly, I want to send a heartfelt thank you to you as well as all of Senior Management who have gone above and beyond to keep all of us healthy and safe during this pandemic. I cannot tell you how proud I am to work for this amazing company that always has the team member at the center of everything and every decision that is made and carried out.

I knew from my first interview over four years ago that this company was something special, and where I wanted to spend the remainder of my working years until retirement.

Thank you for your leadership today and every day!

And this reaction from our Mindfulness coach, Professor Annabel Beerel:

Hello Tom,

What a wonderful email! It is inspiring, touching, and very informative — the perfect communication. Thank you for sharing.

COMMUNICATIONS APPENDIX

To Participating Dentists

Our goal for our first communications with dentists was to reassure them that we were open and ready to serve them:

First Email to Dentists

March 16, 2020

Dear Participating Dentists and Dental Office Teams,

Northeast Delta Dental is closely monitoring developments around the Coronavirus Disease 2019 (COVID-19). Our top priority continues to be the health, safety, and well-being of our subscribers, dentists, producers, employees, and the communities we serve.

We do understand that the Vermont State Dental Society and the Maine Dental Association have issued communications to their members that for the next few weeks, non-essential, non-urgent dental procedures should be suspended.

Please know that our operations are business as usual. We are continuing, and will continue, to process and pay claims, enroll subscribers, and provide the personal service you expect and deserve for those claims and telephone calls we do receive. We have a dedicated response team implementing measures to prevent or minimize any disruptions to our services.

To protect the health of our employees and to ensure that we can continue to meet your needs, we are taking steps to reduce the risk of infection and transmission of COVID-19 among our workforce. These steps include enabling the majority of our employees to work from home, increasing the space between employees who must be at our offices, and reducing or canceling in-person meetings, including on-site HOW® trainings.

We do not anticipate that these steps will cause significant disruptions to our operations. Claims submitted electronically will continue to be processed and paid as quickly as in the past. If you do not currently submit claims electronically and wish to learn more or register to do so, please visit our Electronic Claims Submission website.

This is a rapidly developing situation. We will continue to monitor and follow guidance from the Centers for Disease Control and Prevention and from state and local authorities. We will provide updates if there are any material changes to our ability to meet your needs.

We know that this is a difficult time for everybody. We thank you for your understanding. We hope you, your teams, and your families all remain healthy and well.

Second Email to Dentists

March 22, 2020

Dear Tri-State Participating Dentists and Dental Office Teams,

I trust you and your families, and your dental office teams, are healthy and well.

As you know, there has been a bevy of communications from experts, government agencies, public health officials, the ADA, and our State Dental Societies/Association on a number of topics related to COVID-19. For Northeast Delta Dental's email communications to you on COVID-19 related topics, I will start numbering these so you can refer to them by number, if you have questions for Northeast Delta Dental. This is the third Northeast Delta Dental communication on COVID-19 that has been distributed to all participating dentists in Maine, New Hampshire, and Vermont, although other emails have been distributed state-specific.

Northeast Delta Dental will defer to you, our valued participating dentists, on your interpretations of the professional guidelines, such as what is an emergency. As recent as yesterday's (Saturday afternoon, March 21) White House Coronavirus Task Force press briefing, presenters mentioned that dentists should only be seeing patients with emergencies. We all know that a toothache can turn into an emergency (recall Deamonte Driver), so Northeast Delta Dental leaves that judgment up to you, our professional colleagues. Suffice to say, claims that we receive, electronically or on paper, will be processed. We have a Northeast Delta Dental team on site to process claims and answer telephones (you may wish to look at my video on the Provider Section on the www.nedelta.com website).

I. With regard to teledentistry, much has been written on this topic by public health officials and other insurance companies as a method to help during the COVID -19 crisis. Again, suffice to say, Northeast Delta Dental has paid for services which are benefits under a person's contract, whether provided in person or via teledentistry modes, for some time. We will continue to do so. We will not limit this to the next 90 days as one other carrier referenced. (We also have a major philanthropic initiative in funding teledentistry for underserved children at Boys and Girls Clubs and in schools in New Hampshire, so we have a deep understanding of how this works, and we're committed to the concept if it works for our participating dental offices.)

Because some of our participating dentists may not be familiar with how to bill for services rendered via teledentistry, Northeast Delta Dental will be preparing a "How To" document with the specifics of how to submit claims to us for our covered members. We plan to communicate this to participating dentists during the week of March 23. In the meantime, we encourage participating member dentists to consider submitting claims electronically because we will continue to require a claim form, whether electronic or paper, to adjudicate a claim. While you may have the proper means in place to view a patient's dental condition, either via synchronous or asynchronous modes, you must have a process to submit a claim to Northeast Delta Dental. This may best be done electronically, unless you have easy access to paper claims and a way to complete them. (It's also conceivable the actual physical contact of paper claims and the means to complete them may result in delays due to the threat of possible COVID-19 virus transmission.) In either case, electronic or paper, please use your office address as the treating address for these services.

May I also suggest you consider signing up for electronic payment (EFT) and remittance advices (ERA), in the event there is a disruption in the delivery chain of paper checks. Please contact our Provider Services Department to do this at 603-223-0133.

II. In these trying times, we would like to make it easier for you to receive payments as quickly as possible. While we normally require a dental office to wait until a multi-step procedure (such as a crown) is completed in order to bill Northeast Delta Dental, please take this opportunity to send claim forms to us for any of those services which have been started but not completed. It's possible a service might be denied because the patient has reached his/her maximum, which would not have happened had the claim been submitted when the crown, as an example, was actually placed. In that case, please inform us of the denial and we will reprocess the claim and likely back the amount paid out of the following year's maximum. **Please allow me to stress that this only applies to your patients covered by Northeast Delta Dental.** We cannot authorize payment for multi-step procedures submitted and/or paid for by other Delta Dental Member Companies or any of the commercial carriers, if submitted prior to completion.

Please send questions you may have to Bill Lambrukos (Sr. VP) at Northeast Delta Dental. Bill will compile them for us to review, and we will provide you with future guidance. Bill's email address is wlambrukos@nedelta.com. Please stay well. Thank you!

Example of Encouraging Email at End of 2020

December 20, 2020

Good Sunday Morning Participating Dentists and Dental Office Teams,

As we move closer to year-end, wishing you continued excellent health and a peaceful Holiday season. This Sunday's communication brings the good news that the nitrile gloves have arrived, along with the announcement of a free HPV webinar for which the New Hampshire Dental Society (NHDS) has approved 2.0 CEUs, some year-to-date claim statistics which you might find interesting, and a few reminders.

Northeast Delta Dental PPE Program:

Remember the movie "Miracle on 34th Street"? Well, we had a "Miracle on Two Delta Drive" with the arrival of our first shipment of nitrile gloves in Concord on Tuesday morning! (Please see the attached photograph.) Laureen is working through all of your emails/orders (just like the snow on Thursday, the PPE emails are piling up), and we appreciate your patience as she works through them.

Our strategy is to fill as many glove orders as possible with the inventory and sizes we have available. Our PPE Workshop is a flurry of activity (we now know how Santa and his elves feel) working to get orders packed and shipped as efficiently and quickly as possible. Orders that we are unable to fill at this time will be placed at the top of the glove list for when the next shipment arrives (in January) and filled at that time. Laureen will be in touch with you as she works through the emails and orders.

We continue to have an inventory of multipurpose wipes (75% alcohol), N95 masks, KN95 masks and reusable gowns available as well. Please contact Laureen Drolet at LDrolet@nedelta.com for more information or to obtain a PPE order form.

In addition, in January we will also be distributing free Protective Earloop Facemasks for all 365 Dental Lifeline (aka Donated Dental) volunteer dentists in New Hampshire (157), Maine (158) and Vermont (50). This complimentary PPE is a program sponsored by Dental Lifeline, the supplier DHPI and Northeast Delta Dental, and is just a small token of thanks for these amazing 365 volunteers who have contributed mightily with comprehensive treatment to people with special needs, and veterans, in New Hampshire, Maine, and Vermont.

After about twenty months of weekly communications to our dentists, one Maine dentist summed up his reaction this way:

Dear Tom,

Just wanted to give thanks for the revolution you've created over the past two years. I'm beyond grateful for the time, effort, care, and compassion you've invested in all of us and have no doubt that you've received and will continue to receive much more in return. I pray for your health and that of your entire family.

To Customers

I sent an email letter to our group customers in early March reassuring them we were open (remotely) and paying claims for their employees. We continued to send periodic, reassuring messages in March and April. Then, once we had permission from our Board and our regulators to forgive the customer July premiums, I sent another letter letting them know the good news:

First Constant Contact Mailing to Group Customers

March 18, 2020

Dear Northeast Delta Dental Group Customer, We are closely monitoring developments around the Coronavirus Disease 2019 (COVID-19). Our top priority continues to be the health, safety, and well-being of our subscribers, providers, producers, employees, and the communities we serve.

Please know that our operations are business as usual. We are continuing, and will continue, to process and pay claims, enroll subscribers, and provide the personal service our group customers, subscribers, and dentists expect and deserve. We have a dedicated response team implementing measures to prevent or minimize any disruptions to our services.

To protect the health of our employees and to ensure that we can continue to meet your needs, we are taking steps to reduce the risk of infection and transmission of COVID-19 among our workforce. These steps include enabling the majority of our employees to work from home, increasing the space between employees who must be at our offices, and reducing or canceling in-person meetings.

We do not anticipate that these steps will cause significant disruptions to our operations. This is, however, a rapidly developing situation. We will continue to monitor and follow guidance from the Centers for Disease Control and Prevention and from state and local authorities. We will provide updates if there are any material changes to our ability to meet your needs.

We encourage those who are concerned about access to dental benefits, claims, and other services to contact us at 1-800-537-1715 or nedelta@nedelta.com.

In lieu of our standard Oral Health Update, which is sent periodically via email to several hundred thousand subscribers, we will provide an update on the steps we are taking during the pandemic.

We know that this is a difficult time for everybody, and we will work with our group customers to be flexible in our business dealings. We thank you for your understanding.

Second Constant Contact Mailing to Group Customers

March 23, 2020

Dear Group Customers,

Thank you for all the years you've trusted us to administer the dental benefits of your employees. We appreciate your business.

The COVID-19 pandemic has created a unique set of circumstances. Like many of you, most of our employees are working from home, while some are working from our Concord, New Hampshire, headquarters. We continue to perform all the same processes to serve our stakeholders — efficiently and effectively.

As I said in my video to employers, if you have any issues relating to paying your monthly group premium, we can work with you on that. We have communicated this to your insurance broker or producer. This health crisis calls upon all of us to be more flexible and understanding.

To ensure that our dental networks are available to your employees when they need them, this week Northeast Delta Dental approved a relief package for our currently participating network dentists and oral surgeons. This week, each dental office will receive a check in the amount of approximately one percent of its 2019 claim payments received from Northeast Delta Dental. These funds will not be reflected in the claims experience of our customers and will not impact you negatively.

In addition to the relief package based on 2019 claims payments, claims submitted to Northeast Delta Dental from our PPO providers from mid-February to March 17, 2020, will be adjusted to Premier rates and the amount of the difference between PPO and Premier rates will be calculated and paid in the coming weeks as a second form of relief.

We want our dental office teams to stay healthy and strong so they can continue to be our front line of defense against oral diseases, recognizing that oral health is essential for overall health and well-being.

We wish good health for you, your employees, and your business. If you need to reach customer service, please call 1-800-832-5700. If you have questions for a marketing executive, they can be reached at 1-800-537-1715. To contact me, personally, call 603-223-1300.

Third Constant Contact Mailing to Group Customers

April 15, 2020

Dear Northeast Delta Dental Group Customer,

Northeast Delta Dental continues to monitor the COVID-19 crisis, with our top priority being the health, safety, and well-being of our subscribers, providers, producers, employees, and the communities we serve. The needs of our stakeholders are diverse, and we are doing our very best to balance those needs with any remedy we may have to offer.

As a reminder, it is largely business as usual for us, with most of our employees working from home and a limited number of people working at our office while keeping the recommended distance from each other. We continue to process and pay claims, manage eligibility, and work with our producers and vendors to keep the trains running.

We have studied at length how best to provide relief to our valued customers during this difficult time. In an effort to provide economic relief to our customers renewing during the height of the COVID pandemic, I am happy to announce that Northeast Delta Dental will hold current rates for fully insured group customers renewing July through September.

We are committed to monitoring the crisis and will make any warranted adjustments when and if they are needed. Should you have any questions about this and other customer relief measures we are taking, please do not hesitate to contact your Northeast Delta Dental account manager.

In the calming words of Abraham Lincoln: "When you reach the end of your rope, tie a knot and hang on." We at Northeast Delta Dental are proud to be a small part of your knot. We are all in this together, and together we will persevere.

The individual subscribers received similar letters — personalized with the subscribers' names. In early March, I reassured them we were open. And in April I told the subscribers about forgiving their July premiums:

First *Oral Health Update* Sent to Individual Subscribers

March 19, 2020

Dear Jennifer,

Northeast Delta Dental is closely monitoring developments around the Coronavirus Disease 2019 (COVID-19). Our top priority continues to be the health, safety, and well-being of our subscribers, providers, producers, employees, and the communities we serve.

Please know that our operations are business as usual. We are continuing, and will continue, to process and pay claims, enroll subscribers, and provide the personal service our stakeholders expect and deserve. We have a dedicated response team implementing measures to prevent or minimize any disruptions to our services.

To protect the health of our employees and to ensure that we can continue to meet your needs, we are taking steps to reduce the risk of infection and transmission of COVID-19 among our workforce. These steps include enabling the majority of our employees to work from home, increasing the space between employees who must be at our offices, and reducing or canceling in-person meetings.

We do not anticipate that these steps will cause significant disruptions to our operations. This is, however, a rapidly developing situation. We will continue to monitor and follow guidance from the Centers for Disease Control and Prevention and from state and local authorities. We will provide updates if there are any material changes to our ability to meet your needs.

A Message from the American Dental Association:

In order for dentistry to do its part to mitigate the spread of COVID-19, the American Dental Association (ADA) recommends dentists nationwide postpone elective procedures for the next three weeks. Concentrating on emergency dental care will allow dentists to care for their emergency patients and alleviate the burden that dental emergencies would place on hospital emergency departments. Please visit ADA.org/virus for the latest information.

Second *Oral Health Update* Sent to Individual Subscribers

April 23, 2020

Dear Jennifer,

Northeast Delta Dental continues to monitor the COVID-19 crisis, with our top priority being the health, safety, and well-being of our subscribers, providers, employees, and the communities we serve. The needs of our stakeholders are diverse, and we are doing our very best to balance those needs with any remedy we may have to offer.

As a reminder, it is largely business as usual for us, with most of our employees working from home and a limited number of people working at our office while keeping the recommended distance from each other. We continue to process and pay claims, manage enrollments, and provide world-class customer service.

The COVID pandemic has caused disruption and uncertainty in our daily lives, but worrying about your Northeast Delta Dental coverage should not be an additional stress for you. We have implemented measures to ensure that potential disruptions to your coverage are minimized, and that should you be furloughed, you can continue your coverage or easily have it restored upon your return to work.

As a reminder, many dental offices are open to treat dental emergencies during this time. Should you have an emergency, please contact your regular dentist or another local dentist if your regular dental office is closed. Please try to avoid using the emergency room for dental-related issues.

Stay strong. Be safe. We are all in this together, and together we will persevere.

Public Blogs, Op-Eds, and Radio

I also did several radio spots (WGIR and Binnie Media) and wrote a number of blogs and op-eds (e.g., 7/20/2020 *Union Leader* and 8/18/2020 *Concord Monitor*) reassuring our subscribers and the public that it was safe to return to their dentists for treatment:

Dental offices reopening: Heroes work here!

Posted on July 2, 2020, by neddblog

Have you seen the signs thanking heroes emerging during the COVID-19 pandemic? I haven't seen one listing dental professionals, but I think they should be included. Outside of every dental office a sign should appear that says, "Heroes Work Here!" When you consider that the disease is spread through small droplets from the nose and mouth, and where and how dentists and dental auxiliary staff work, the risk factors of dental health care professionals approach those of other medical care professionals — or exceed them!

On March 16, the American Dental Association (ADA) recommended that dental offices close to all but urgent and emergency dental care. After several weeks of being unavailable for all elective procedures, most dentists are back to business, following the recommendations of the ADA, CDC, and their state departments of health and safety to ensure the safety of their patients and staff.

During the period when dental offices were closed, teledentistry helped patients with a dental emergency access the expertise of their dentist via HIPAA-compliant live video conferences to triage the problems and discuss next steps. Teledentistry visits can often alleviate patient anxiety and eliminate a trip to the emergency room. Many dental insurance companies appreciate the role played by teledentistry and reimburse for teledentistry procedures, and many dentists have added teledentistry as a service option. Dr. Bryan Hoertdoerfer, of Hoertdoerfer Dentistry, Manchester, says, 'We have incorporated teledentistry as an option within our business. Teledentistry is here to stay."

Dental offices are inherently health- and safety-conscious; even so, if you've visited your dentist's office since they've reopened, you've seen several changes because of the pandemic. Because dental offices have been closed, you might have to wait a bit longer for an appointment, so schedule one soon. If you haven't visited since they've reopened, here are some changes you can expect.

You may be screened for COVID-19 symptoms during your appointment call, and you may be asked similar questions the day of your dental visit. Some dental offices may want you to answer those questions outside of the office, or as soon as you walk in. Your temperature may be taken. You will most likely be asked to wear a mask, which you can remove in the dental chair. You may be asked to wait in your car and call when you arrive rather than waiting in the waiting room; in the waiting room, you may see fewer chairs and no toys or magazines. Visitors are unlikely to be welcomed, with the possible exception of one parent with a young child. You may be asked to use hand sanitizer. You may hear the hum of air purifiers. You may see office areas shielded, and dentists and dental auxiliary staff (dental hygienists and assistants) wearing more personal protective equipment than usual.

Dental office safety is a joint responsibility, so please reschedule your appointment if you develop symptoms, test positively for COVID-19, or are exposed to someone with COVID-19 to protect the dental health professionals who are protecting you.

Northeast Delta Dental is pleased to have been able to support our participating dentists with PPE and financial relief while dental offices are closed, and now as they reopen. To learn more, visit www.nedelta.com.

The public needs all its healthcare heroes during the current health crisis.

Posted on August 13, 2020, by neddblog:

The World Health Organization (WHO) recently issued interim guidance on providing essential oral health services in the context of COVID-19, advocating that preventive dental care be delayed until there has been sufficient reduction in transmission rates.

The American Dental Association (ADA); Delta Dental Plans Association (39 Member Companies); Northeast Delta Dental; the Boards of Dental Examiners in Maine, New Hampshire and Vermont and other dental industry leaders at the state and national levels respectfully disagree with WHO's position on preventive care during the current health crisis.

The WHO is a worldwide organization. Its interim guidance does not account for differences in safety practices and equipment around the world. In the United States, the ADA did recommend in March that dental practices suspend preventive care and focus on emergency procedures to mitigate the spread of COVID-19 and alleviate the burden that dental emergencies would place on hospital emergency departments.

Thereafter, the ADA, in conjunction with the Centers for Disease Control (CDC), developed rigorous safety, equipment and practice protocols designed to protect patients, dentists and dental auxiliary staff. In each state, local Boards of Dental Examiners presented these protocols to state reopening taskforces for recommendation to, and approval by, state government. State governments only permitted dental offices to reopen for preventive care when they were satisfied that dental offices could do so safely.

Dental offices are again open and providing a full range of dental services that are critical to the health and wellbeing of their patients. They follow safety protocols that are much more rigorous than usual, though dental offices are safety-conscious in the best of times. Many thousands of people nationwide have received routine dental procedures in the last few months without incident. The Journal of the American Dental Association (JADA) will document this more fully in an article in its upcoming issue.

On the topic of its interim guidance, one of WHO's dental officers was quoted as saying, "We think that the most pressing issue is related to the availability of essential personal protective equipment, PPE, for all health care personnel undertaking or assisting in the clinical procedures." We agree. That's why Northeast Delta Dental has distributed tens of thousands of masks and thousands of gowns to our network dentists and is helping them with the ongoing costs of PPE and other COVID-19 expenses.

As they plan their next visits, we encourage patients to contact their dentists to learn more about specific protocols in place for health and safety. Dental professionals are on the front lines of health care, with their expertise often detecting, and/or impacting, such diseases as diabetes, heart disease, and cancer. Let's not limit our healthcare system's ability to treat the whole patient by discouraging people from visiting their dentists, when both national and state public health authorities have determined that they can do so safely.

To Brokers and Benefit Consultants

My first emailed letter to the brokers and benefit consultants went out in March and generally reassured them that we were open for (remote) business and would be available to them. In our second email in April, we reassured them that we would hold rates steady. By May, we had approval to forgive group and individual customer premiums, so our third communication let the brokers know the details of how they would still receive their payments.

First Constant Contact Mailing to Brokers and Benefit Consultants

March 18, 2020

Dear Northeast Delta Dental Producer,

We are closely monitoring developments around the Coronavirus Disease 2019 (COVID-19). Our top priority continues to be the health, safety, and well-being of our subscribers, providers, producers, employees, and the communities we serve.

Please know that our operations are business as usual. We are continuing, and will continue, to process and pay claims, enroll subscribers, and provide the personal service our stakeholders expect and deserve. We have a dedicated response team implementing measures to prevent or minimize any disruptions to our services.

To protect the health of our employees and to ensure that we can continue to meet your needs, we are taking steps to reduce the risk of infection and transmission of COVID-19 among our workforce. These steps include enabling the majority of our employees to work from home, increasing the space between employees who must be at our offices, and reducing or canceling in-person meetings.

We do not anticipate that these steps will cause significant disruptions to our operations. This is, however, a rapidly developing situation. We will continue to monitor and follow guidance from the Centers for Disease Control and Prevention and from state and local authorities. We will provide updates if there are any material changes to our ability to meet your needs.

We encourage those who are concerned about access to dental benefits, claims, and other services to contact us at 1-800-537-1715 or nedelta@nedelta.com.

We know that this is a difficult time for everybody, and we will work with our groups, your clients, and be flexible in our business dealings. We thank you for your understanding.

Second Constant Contact Mailing to Brokers and Benefit Consultants

April 15, 2020

Dear Northeast Delta Dental Producer,

Northeast Delta Dental continues to monitor the COVID-19 crisis, with our top priority being the health, safety, and well-being of our subscribers, providers, producers, employees, and the communities we serve. The needs of our stakeholders are diverse, and we are doing our very best to balance those needs with any remedy we may have to offer.

As a reminder, it is largely business as usual for us, with most of our employees working from home and a limited number of people working at our office while keeping the recommended distance from each other. We continue to process and pay claims, manage eligibility, and work with our producers and vendors to keep the trains running.

We have studied at length how best to provide relief to our valued customers during this difficult time. In an effort to provide economic relief to our customers renewing during the height of the COVID pandemic, I am happy to announce that Northeast Delta Dental will hold current rates for fully insured group customers renewing July through September. Again, this is for fully insured group customers only and does not apply to self-insured customers' plans that are intrinsically tied to relief as claims volume lessens. Please provide this information to others with whom you work so that they are also up to speed with our relief efforts. Thank you.

We are committed to monitoring the crisis and will make any warranted adjustments when and if they are needed. Should you have any questions about this and other customer relief measures we are taking, please do not hesitate to contact your Northeast Delta Dental account manager.

Third Constant Contact Mailing to Brokers and Benefit Consultants

May 15, 2020

Dear Northeast Delta Dental Producer,

As communicated in my last email to you, Northeast Delta Dental has studied at length how best to provide relief to our valued customers during this difficult time. In an effort to provide economic relief to our customers renewing during the height of the COVID-19 pandemic, I am happy to announce that Northeast Delta Dental has extended rate holds for fully insured group customers renewing July through December. Again, this is for fully insured group customers only.

Additionally, I am happy to announce that Northeast Delta Dental will be providing all fully insured individual and group customers a one-month dental premium credit in July based on June's billed amount.

Premium credit details for fully insured customers:

They can locate the amount due for July (with the credit applied) in the CURRENT MONTH BILLED field on the Remittance Page of the July bill.

If the credit is greater than the amount of the July invoice, the additional credit will be applied to future invoices until the full credit has been exhausted Any retroactivity will still be reflected within the July invoice, just as it is every month.

This is a one-time credit. There will be no retroactive refunds reflected on future invoices.

For all fully-insured group customers that receive their Northeast Delta Dental bills via our eBilling portal, the amount due for July with the credit applied will be displayed in the last (Balance) column on the Dashboard.

We will also be offering relief to self-insured customers. Claim reimbursements to Northeast Delta Dental have been significantly lower since COVID-19 forced the closure of most dental practices (except for dental emergencies). Self-insured customers' plans are intrinsically tied to savings from decreased claims volumes that will likely be slow to return to pre-pandemic levels.

Notwithstanding savings from lower dental claim payments, we realize that many of our self-insured customers have been financially impacted in other ways. Like Northeast Delta Dental, most businesses have ongoing overhead expenses during a time when income levels may have been diminished.

We are pleased to announce that we will be crediting the July administrative fee for all of our self-insured customers.

Administrative fee credit details for self-insured customers:

Northeast Delta Dental will credit the July administrative fee for their July invoice.

The July bill will still calculate and issue the administrative fee but the amount due will be $0.00. When the July month-end bills are posted to the eBilling portal, they will see $0.00 due in the Balance column on the Dashboard, which is the last column. This is a one-time credit. There will be no retroactive refunds reflected on future invoices.

Finally, we understand that you may also be impacted financially by the pandemic. For that reason, Northeast Delta Dental will pay commissions during the premium/admin credit period. Our group customer commissions are based on premiums and administrative fees billed, and our Individual and Family (IAF) commissions are based on premiums received, which means your commissions would otherwise be $0.00 or significantly reduced. Your commissions for the month of July (paid in August) will be the same as your commissions for the month of June (paid in July). We are happy we are able to maintain your income from Northeast Delta Dental during this difficult time. Thank you for your continued partnership.

As previously stated, we are committed to monitoring the crisis and will make any warranted adjustments when and if they are needed. Per usual, should you have any questions about this and other customer relief measures we are taking, please do not hesitate to contact your Northeast Delta Dental account manager.

The following comment was received from a broker after an October 2021 Zoom meeting with dentists, group customers and the broker community:

> Hi Tom and Jodie,
>
> Thanks again for letting me be a part of this group.
>
> Until the meeting, I didn't realize how much reimbursement Northeast Delta Dental had done for the Dental Providers.
>
> I would say I am surprised, but I am really not. When your providers needed help, you stepped right up.
>
> So indirectly, as a broker who has several Dental office clients in New Hampshire, thanks for helping them stay in business during a really tough time.

Northeast Delta Dental's commitment to supporting the annual Black New England Conference is reflected in the following letter:

Message from the Black Heritage Trail of New Hampshire Executive Director

November 2021

> It is with gratitude and full hearts that we enter this season of giving thanks. The Black Heritage Trail of New Hampshire continues to grow as more and more people and organizations respond to our invitation to join a safe space for dialogue and learning about race — both virtually and in person. As we continue to grapple with our troubled legacy of inequality, racial division, and divisive concept legislation in New Hampshire, Black Heritage Trail of New Hampshire recognizes it is essential to continue to share the complete and unvarnished history of the African American experience.
>
> This past year, we created new markers for black history in New Hampshire. The new Hancock marker describes the Due family and Jack, a once enslaved African who gained his freedom and lived in Hancock in the late 1700s and early 1800s. The new marker in Warner commemorates four black men who served as soldiers in three different wars and represent a part of the rich history of Warner's black community. Our partnership with New Hampshire Forest Society brought together people from many different backgrounds to do what

we do best — present new corrective narratives of our history that challenge stereotypes and build new understanding of our diverse community.

The 15th Annual Black New England Conference in October attracted speakers and participants from around the country who engaged in deep and meaningful conversation and learning together. **As Tom Raffio, President and CEO of Northeast Delta Dental wrote in his note of thanks, "The Black New England Conference was compelling, educational, inspirational, and authentic. I'm convinced that while the journey is a journey without a finish line, and that we have a long way to go, that the more we dialogue, the more we will progress."**

Together we will promote awareness and appreciation of New Hampshire's African American history and life, and build more inclusive communities throughout New Hampshire. We hope you'll include Black Heritage Trail of New Hampshire in your year-end giving.

Wishing you and yours a happy Thanksgiving,

JerriAnne Boggis, Executive Director
Black Heritage Trail of New Hampshire

Acknowledgements

Tom Raffio's Acknowledgements

It truly takes a team to write a meaningful book that people will read with a smile. Starting with my amazing co-author, Diane Schmalensee, I'd also like to thank past and present colleagues of Northeast Delta Dental, including Betty Andrews, Richard Tango-Lowy, Sara Brehm, Mike Paulin, Alex Berube, and Jennifer McGrath, who provided helpful suggestions along the way. Thanks to our graphics colleagues Steven Foley (who patiently worked many late nights with me on the book production), Cyndi Carr, and Jim Hendrix.

I'd also like to thank early manuscript readers Dr. David Staples, Chair of Delta Dental Plan of New Hampshire; the esteemed Dr. Sylvio Dupuis, former President of Notre Dame College and Catholic Medical Center; John Gladden, President and CEO of Delta Dental of Oklahoma; Craig Goldsmith, DeltaVision® Project/Product Manager; and Dale Dewey, serial entrepreneur. Of course, a big thank you to all employee and Board member colleagues of Northeast Delta Dental, without whom our processes and results could not have been realized.

Thank you to Dr. Bob Hunter, former President & CEO of Delta Dental of Massachusetts who was a role model leader when I was VP there and whose approaches then helped me during this pandemic.

Much gratitude to media and radio/TV colleagues Chris Ryan, Jack Heath (also an author), Ken Cail, Peter St. James, Jamie Staton, Mike Morin, and the eclectic Scott Spradling. Thanks to Baldrige experts and ExcellenceNorth Alliance colleagues, Anne Warner and Brian Hettrick, and to University of New Hampshire President, Dr. James Dean, who recognizes the importance of the Baldrige performance framework.

The work of Will Arvelo and Jermaine Moore, who help lead New Hampshire's DEI efforts, should be noted — they have helped Northeast Delta Dental and me so much. Ali Sekou Diallo, President of the Islamic Society of Greater Concord and a colleague and mentee, has also led local DEI initiatives.

Northeast Delta Dental's wonderful partnership with the NH Fisher Cats, personified in owner Art Solomon and Team President Mike Ramshaw, should also be recognized as this partnership helps our community outreach outlined in the book.

Our partnerships with Joan Benoit Samuelson and the Beach to Beacon 10K Road Race and with former DDPME Board Members, Dr. Barry Saltz and Dr. Fred Bechard, have also paid dividends for the Maine communities in which we operate.

Role models for mental health awareness — former NH Supreme Court Chief Justice John Broderick, Life Coach Jeff Levin, and the team at Seacoast United — helped design Northeast Delta Dental's wellness initiatives mentioned in this book. Much of the work that Northeast Delta Dental does in the Veterans community, referenced in this book, resulted from special people such as Larry Gammon (former Easterseals New Hampshire President & CEO), Jack Heath, Dr. Mitch Couret, Phil Taub, Esq., David Tille, and Nancy and Bill Marston, who partnered with us and called the Veterans' oral health and other needs to our attention.

An additional thank you to David Audet, Hall of Fame Runner (one of only a handful of runners who have run an under three-hour marathon in all 50 states), and his mother, Janet Muller, who provided inspiration as we traveled together to various road races across Northern New England, and positive feedback on my earlier two books at coffee stops after races. She encouraged me to write this third book. Boston Marathon Race Director and fearless runner, Dave McGillivary, and iron heart Jeremy Woodward were additional sources of inspiration.

Seasoned mentors Dr. Henry Plodzik, Dr. Robert Fremeau, Fred Phinney, and Tom Walton (also my wellness coach) also provided much-needed encouragement and support.

Final shout-outs to John Jay Bonstingl, education and leadership consultant, whose quality philosophies helped shape my thinking and actions during the height of the pandemic, along with Retired Brigadier General, Attorney Bob Dastin, whose mentorship since 1995 has been invaluable, and insightful professional colleagues David Germain and Steve Duprey.

It's not lost on me that my leadership style, which has worked so well throughout my professional career and particularly during the pandemic, was shaped by growing up with four amazing sisters and my mother. They still Zoom with me on a biweekly basis and provide constant positive reinforcement. Thanks to them for saying that my community engagement reminds them of our departed father and husband.

I thank my four grown children, Jenna, Matt, Brian, and Gabbie, for becoming outstanding leaders in their own careers and families and for many meaningful conversations about leading Millennials. (Trust me — Millennials like my children work as hard and want to contribute as much as any generation!) A note of gratitude to Soccer Coach George Pinkham for mentoring Brian.

Finally, and importantly, a huge thank you to my lovely wife Ellen, who gave me the support and encouragement needed to lead Delta Dental, serve on external Boards, and write this book with Diane.

As this goes to press, Mike Paulin, Digital Content Coordinator, aka "The Web Guy", and a beloved employee, has just passed away. All of us at Northeast Delta Dental thank him for his nearly 20 years of service. As this issue of *Team Power* says, Mike will be greatly missed.

Diane Schmalensee's Acknowledgements

A huge thank you to Tom Raffio for being the inspiring leader and person that he is. I've been honored to work with Tom for nearly 30 years and have never failed to be impressed and gladdened by the experience. This is the third book that I've helped Tom write, and I believe it's his best because it offers so much of the wisdom he has gained over the years.

Thank you also to the many people of Northeast Delta Dental who make up such a dedicated team and who are always a pleasure to work with.

Thanks also to Len Berry, University Distinguished Professor of Marketing, Mays Business School, Texas A&M University, and to Kay Kendall, Principal of Baldrige Coach, for their very helpful reviews of the book.

And a very loving thanks to my husband, Richard Schmalensee, and our sons, Alex and Nick, for supporting me in so many ways during the writing of this book and throughout our lives together.

About the Authors

Thomas Raffio, President & CEO
Northeast Delta Dental
One Delta Drive, Concord, NH 03302-2002
TomRaffio@nedelta.com
603-223-1000

Career History

Thomas Raffio is President & CEO of Northeast Delta Dental, a role he has held since 1995. Before that, he was Senior Vice President of Delta Dental of Massachusetts and Director of Group Healthcare Management Reporting at John Hancock Insurance.

Accomplishment Highlights

- Grew Northeast Delta Dental from administering the dental benefits of 300,000 people in its tri-state region to over 950,000.
- Increased revenue from $57 million to over $344 million.
- Created the Guarantee Of Service Excellence℠ (GOSE℠) program, backing up seven facets of service with customer refunds — the first such comprehensive program in Northern New England.
- Grew the enterprise from ~50 to ~200 employees, earning a reputation as "Employer of Choice" based on best practices and numerous awards.
- Increased its strong network of participating dentists by growth from 935 to 1,810.
- Spearheaded the creation of the Northeast Delta Dental Foundation, which supports oral health programs in Maine, New Hampshire, and Vermont each year by investing several hundred thousand dollars.

Civic Roles

Tom is an engaged civic leader. He is currently a member of the Board of Trustees of Dartmouth-Hitchcock, member of the Delta Dental Plans Association Board of Directors, Chair of the New Hampshire Coalition for Business and Education, Chair of the Arthritis Leadership Council of Northern New England, a member of the Business and Industry Association, a Board member and former Chair of the Board of Early Learning New Hampshire, Chair of the Franklin Pierce College of Business Advisory Board, and a member of the Conference Board's Committee for Economic Development. He is Incorporator and Chair of the Board of ExcellenceNorth Alliance, Board member and Chair of New Hampshire Business Committee for the Arts, Chair of the Bow Schools Foundation, member of the New Hampshire Scholars Leadership Board — which he also serves as a Champion — an active Big Brother for Big Brothers Big Sisters of New Hampshire, and member of the Fisher Cats Foundation. Tom served as former Chair of the New Hampshire State Board of Education, former Chair of the New Hampshire Symphony Orchestra, and former member of the New Hampshire Historical Society's Democracy Project Advisory Committee.

Publications

- "The Baldrige and I," *Baldrige Foundation Institute for Performance Excellence White Paper* 2021-01, May 15, 2021.
- Annabel C. Beerel and Tom Raffio, *Mindfulness: A Better Me; a Better You; a Better World*. Self, 2018.
- Tom Raffio with Barbara McLaughlin and Dave Cowens, *There Are No Do-Overs: The Big Red Factors for Sustaining a Business Long Term*. Curran Pendleton Press, 2013.

Education

Tom earned an undergraduate degree at Harvard University, an MBA from Babson College, and designation as a Fellow of the Life Management Institute (FLMI). He graduated from the Leadership New Hampshire Class of 1997, and is thankful that Dr. Stephen Reno keeps this program thriving.

Family

Tom lives in Bow, New Hampshire, with his wife, Ellen; three stepdaughters, Margaret, Sophie, and Annika; granddaughter, Havanna; German Shepherd, Kolton; Labrador Retriever, Vincent; and two cats, Scout and Jack. Tom has four adult children from a previous marriage, Jenna, Matt, Brian, and Gabrielle, and two granddaughters, Hannah and Ruthie.

ABOUT THE AUTHORS

Diane H. Schmalensee, President
Schmalensee Partners
172 Beacon Street – Boston, MA 02116
diane@schmalensee.com
617-247-0045 (O) or 617-835-9405 (M)

Career History

Diane Schmalensee is President of Schmalensee Partners, which she founded in 1991. Before that, she was Vice President of Service Excellence for Opinion Research Corporation and Vice President of Research for the Marketing Science Institute.

Accomplishment Highlights

Diane helps service organizations of all sizes and types (including educational, healthcare, governmental, and private organizations) to improve customer experiences and build loyalty and revenues through performance excellence. She specializes in listening to internal and external stakeholders and using proven management tools such as the Baldrige principles to boost outcomes and results.

Award-winning clients include AT&T (American Transtech Florida Award Winner and Universal Card Baldrige Winner), Clark & Reid (Massachusetts Award Winner), Datatel-Now Ellucian (Virginia Award Winner), Delta Dental of Massachusetts (Massachusetts Award Winner), and Northeast Delta Dental (winner of many awards as an employer and corporate citizen).

Diane speaks and publishes on service quality, customer loyalty, strategic planning, and performance measurement for associations, such as The Conference Board, the American Marketing Association, and the American Society for Quality, as well as for corporations. She worked on two previous books with Tom Raffio, including *There Are No Do-Overs* and *Mindfulness: A Better Me, a Better You, a Better World*.

Civic Roles

Diane is an eight-time Examiner for the Malcolm Baldrige National Quality Award and was a judge, trainer, and officer of the Massachusetts quality award (now called Partners in Performance Excellence) from 1992 to 2017. She served on the Editorial Review Boards of *Marketing Research Magazine* and *Marketing Management*. She is a Board member (now Chair Emerita) since 2000 and past chair (2005-2007) of the Pioneer Institute for Public Policy and has been an Advisor for the Boston Ballet since 2008. In addition, she has served as Vice Chair on the Board of MassBay Community College and is a Board Member of Max Warburg Courage Curriculum and the Chilton Club. She has served on the Board of Nichols College, the Association for Consumer Research, the American Marketing Association, and the U.S. Census.

Publications

- "Building Customer Loyalty, Corporate Reputation, and Shareholder Value Through Service Quality Improvement and Internal Customer Satisfaction" in *Managing Service Quality*.
- "Finding the 'Perfect' Scale" in *Marketing Research*.
- "Lessons Learned on Our Quality Journey" in *The Center for Quality Management Journal*.
- "Unleashing the Power of Connecting Disciplines" in *Reflections*.
- "Rules of Thumb for B2B Research", "Measuring Returns on Research", "Creating Win-Win Relationships", and "How to Make Research More Actionable" in *Marketing Research*. This last article won the Dave Hardin prize for the best article of the year from the American Marketing Association.

Education

Diane earned a BA from Wellesley College and an MBA from San Diego State University, with a concentration in Marketing and Marketing Research.

Family

Diane is blessed with a loving and close-knit family. She lives in Boston with her husband, the economist, Richard Schmalensee. They have two grown sons. The older, Alex Schmalensee, lives in Hawaii with his wife, Juyeon, and two children, Kylie'ena and Kullum. The younger, Nick Schmalensee, lives in the Boston area with his wife, Lizzie, and their two children, Beatrix, and Hazel. She misses her beloved beagle, Freckles.

References Mentioned in This Book

- *2021-2022 Baldrige Excellence Framework (Business/Nonprofit).* National Institute of Standards and Technology (NIST), December 2020.
- Rod Adner, *The Wide Lens: A New Strategy for Innovation.* Penguin Group, 2012.
- *Baldrige Excellence Framework.* Published annually by the Baldrige Performance Excellence Program within the National Institute of Standards and Technology since 1987. There are three versions: 1- Business, Service, Small Business, Nonprofit/Government; 2- Healthcare; and 3- Education.
- John M. Barry, *The Great Influenza: The Story of the Deadliest Pandemic in History.* Penguin Books, 2005.
- Annabel C. Beerel and Tom Raffio, *Mindfulness: A Better Me; a Better You; a Better World.* Self, 2018.
- Leonard L. Berry and Rana Lee Adawi Awdish, "Health Care Organizations Should Be as Generous as Their Workers," *Annals of Internal Medicine*, January 2021.
- Jim Collins, *Good to Great: Why Some Companies Make the Leap and Others Don't.* HarperBusiness, 2001.
- Committee for Economic Development of The Conference Board, "Vaccinating America," *Sustaining Capitalism Series*, April 6, 2021.
- Max De Pree, *Leadership Is an Art.* Crown/Archetype, 2004.
- Daniel DeFoe, *A Journal of the Plague Year.* Norton Critical Editions (Paula R. Backscheider, Editor), 1992 based on original of 1722.
- Scott Galloway, *Post Corona: From Crisis to Opportunity.* Portfolio, 2020.
- Glassdoor White Paper. *Culture Over Cash? Glassdoor Multi-Country Survey Finds More than Half of Employees Prioritize Workplace Culture Over Salary.* July 10, 2019.
- Robert Greenleaf, *The Power of Servant Leadership.* Berrett-Koehler, 1998.

- Harvard Business School Course, "Making Corporate Boards More Effective—Board Governance".
- Harry Hertz, "Regaining Trust: Lead with Facts, Listen and Act with Empathy," *The Baldrige Cheermudgeon on Blogrige*, March 25, 2021. (www.nist.gove/blogs/blogrige/authors/harry-hertz)
- Ira Kalish, Michael Wolf, and Jonathan Holdowsky, "The Link Between Trust and Economic Prosperity," *Deloitte Insights*, May 20, 2021.
- John Kay and Mervyn King, *Radical Uncertainty*. The Bridge Street Press, 2020.
- Kay Kendall and Glenn Bodinson, *Leading the Malcolm Baldrige Way: How World-Class Leaders Align Their Organizations to Deliver Exceptional Results*. McGraw-Hill Education, 2016.
- Bill Koenigsberg, "Resetting a Culture for the New Abnormal," *Chief Executive CEO Briefing*, November 1, 2021.
- Mark Barr McClellan, "Insights for What's Ahead-Understanding the Delta Variant," Committee for Economic Development of The Conference Board, *Sustaining Capitalism Series*, July 30, 2021.
- Douglas McGregor, *The Human Side of Enterprise*. McGraw-Hill, 1960.
- Mary Otto, *Teeth: The Story of Beauty, Inequality, and the Struggle for Oral Health in America*. The New Press, 2017.
- PricewaterhouseCoopers, PwC U.S. Pulse Survey, *CHROs Bet on Inclusion to Retain Talent and Launch Hybrid Work*, August 19, 2021
- Prevedere White Paper, *American Workers' Viewpoint: The New Link Between Personal Job Security and Corporate Business Plans*. June 2021.
- Tom Raffio, "The Baldrige and I," *Baldrige Foundation Institute for Performance Excellence White Paper 2021-01*, May 15, 2021. Also, *Journal of Performance Excellence*, 2020/2021 Issue.
- Tom Raffio with Barbara McLaughlin and Dave Cowens, *There Are No Do-Overs: The Big Red Factors for Sustaining a Business Long Term*. Curran Pendleton Press, 2013.
- Jim Schleckser, "Why Using Force Doesn't Work in Business or in Life," Inc. CEO Project Blog, August 10, 2021.
- George Shultz Opinion, "The Most Important Things I've Learned About Trust Over My 100 Years," *The Washington Post*, December 10, 2020.

REFERENCES MENTIONED IN THIS BOOK

- John Tschohl, *Relentless*. Best Sellers Publishing, 2020.
- Paul Zak, "The Neuroscience of Trust," *Harvard Business Review*, January 1, 2017.
- Jack Zenger and Joseph Folkman, "The Three Elements of Trust," *Harvard Business Review*, February 5, 2019.
- Jack Zenger and Joseph Folkman, "Research: Women Are Better Leaders During a Crisis," *Harvard Business Review*, December 30, 2020